THE DESTINY OF THE MOTHER CHURCH

" THE SHADOW OF A GREAT ROCK."

Copyright 1898.
Jas. F. Gilman.

" AND THE RAIN DESCENDED, AND THE FLOODS CAME AND THE WINDS BLEW,
AND BEAT UPON THAT HOUSE; AND IT FELL NOT; FOR IT WAS FOUNDED UPON A ROCK."

Mary Baker G. Eddy and James F. Gilman, Artists*

*Original Caption

THE DESTINY OF

THE MOTHER CHURCH

By
Bliss Knapp

———————*———————

 THE CHRISTIAN SCIENCE PUBLISHING SOCIETY
BOSTON, MASSACHUSETTS, U.S.A.

ISBN: 0-87510-231-X
Library of Congress Catalog Card No. 91-75317

Printed in the United States of America

INTRODUCTION:
TWENTIETH-CENTURY BIOGRAPHERS SERIES

In the closing years of the twentieth century, there is a growing awareness that the hundred years since 1900 will have registered a magnitude and pace of change, in every aspect of human affairs, which probably exceeds any historic precedent. In political, social and religious institutions and attitudes, in the sciences and industry, in the arts, in how we communicate with each other, humanity has traveled light years in this century.

"Earth's actors," said the Founder of Christian Science, Mary Baker Eddy, "change earth's scenes . . . ." As we look back over the landscape of this century, some towering figures emerge into view: political leaders, scientists and inventors, authors, artists and musicians, social and religious pioneers, industrialists, and many others who helped "change earth's scenes."

Typically, when someone comes along who changes human perceptions and ways of acting, he or she attracts biographers. If an individual career is perceived, with growing distance, to have been especially significant in its impact on human affairs and changing ideas, the shelf of biography steadily expands; and each new published work, even though it may cover some of the ground already treated in earlier works, is expected to bring further insight into the meaning of a life, a mind, and a career.

Even among those who are not her followers, Mary Baker Eddy is customarily regarded as a major religious figure of the twentieth century and as a notable example of the emergence of women in significant leadership roles. Her works are visible today in virtually every country of the world: in church buildings, in Christian Science Reading Rooms, in the distribution of the newspaper and religious periodicals she established and their derivative broadcast forms, in the wide circulation of her own writings, and most important, in the way hundreds of thousands of people conduct their everyday lives.

Public interest in Mrs. Eddy, and curiosity about her, are as strong today as they were in 1910, the year of her decease. And yet, compared with other major figures of the century, the shelf of biography has increased little in the intervening years. A handful of early biographies, by those who knew her or stood close to her in time, were augmented in the late 1960s by Robert Peel's monumental three-volume work. Most of those early works, in spite of their great value as part of the historical record, have lapsed from print; and in fact some first-hand reminiscences by individuals who worked directly with her have only been privately published or circulated.

As we near the close of a century which directly witnessed some of Mary Baker Eddy's major contributions,

The Christian Science Publishing Society, the publishing arm of the church she established, has reexamined the church's obligations to future generations and centuries, in providing an appreciation and understanding of her remarkable career.

Mrs. Eddy wrote only briefly about herself, in a short volume titled *Retrospection and Introspection*. She discouraged personal adulation or attention, clearly hoping that people would find her character and purpose in her own writings rather than in the biographic record. Yet, she came to see the need for an accurate account of her life and gave specific if possibly reluctant acquiescence in the year 1910 to the publishing of the first of the biographies — Sybil Wilbur's *Mary Baker Eddy*.

In addition to Robert Peel's trilogy, which is still in print, a number of significant biographic resources must remain, or become, permanently and readily available to future generations. These include: first-hand recollections of early workers who served directly under her leadership, not all of which have yet been published; and the various biographies which have already won their place in the history of Christian Science and in public use.

For these reasons, the Publishing Society welcomes the opportunity of publishing, and keeping in print, a major shelf of works on Mary Baker Eddy under the general series title: "Twentieth-Century Biographers Series."

Although a consistent set of editorial standards has been applied to such elements as indexing and footnoting, where required, with regard to dates, events, and statements of fact, the original texts of the authors have been preserved intact.

If the reader finds, through these volumes, occasional differing interpretations of events or concepts, this should serve as a strength rather than a weakness in a record which is so clearly synoptical in nature. Especially in the case of those who worked directly with Mrs. Eddy and shared many of her experiences, a special measure of respect and textual integrity is demanded. These are the workers she chose — individuals who served as her lieutenants, often for many years. To describe them as sturdy, strong-minded workers, patriarchal in their devotion and self-sacrifice, scarcely does them justice.

Mrs. Eddy's career and works have stirred humanity in the twentieth century and will continue to do so. Perhaps an appropriate introduction for this series is captured in her statement, in the Preface to *Science and Health with Key to the Scriptures:* "The time for thinkers has come."

In that spirit, this series of biographies by many different twentieth-century writers is offered to all those who, now and in the future, want to know more about this remarkable woman, her life, and her work.

FOREWORD

BLISS KNAPP was first introduced to Mary Baker Eddy when she was a guest in the home of his parents in the summer of 1888. Sometime later, she requested his parents to give him a college education. It was while he was still a senior at Harvard College that Mrs. Eddy made him a First Member of her Church. Before he had been out of college three years, she made him a member of the Board of Lectureship, and sent him a little book on elocution to study. She carefully edited one of his lectures, and wrote the following letter concerning it:

Addressed to Bliss Knapp

> Pleasant View,
> Concord, N. H.
> Sept. 10, 1906.

Beloved Student:

I have read carefully your lecture — made a few changes and I pronounce it *excellent*. You have followed in the letter and in the spirit my writings and teachings very closely, and must be a good practitioner, if you realize what you write even in a small degree. I am exceedingly rejoiced at the prospect of your prosperity in truth and love divine.

I want you to publish this lecture in a pamphlet and send it over this planet.

In haste

> your loving friend,
> (*Signed*) MARY BAKER EDDY.

Later, Mrs. Eddy asked to have that lecture translated into French, the first Christian Science literature to be translated into a foreign language.

Mr. Knapp continued to serve on the Board of Lectureship for about twenty-one years, and for a period of seven years he was its executive secretary, succeeding William P. McKenzie, who was the first to hold that office. Mr. Knapp also served as President, Treasurer, and First Reader of The Mother Church, and as Chairman of the Bible Lesson Committee.

The first part of this volume contains a revision of the book which Bliss Knapp published in 1925, and he takes this opportunity to express his deep gratitude to his dear wife, Eloise Mabury Knapp, who has so ably coöperated with him in producing this book.

Brookline, Massachusetts, 1947.

CONTENTS

Contents

I

TWO OF MRS. EDDY'S CHURCH BUILDERS

CHAPTER I

*

Two of Mrs. Eddy's Church Builders

MARY BAKER EDDY selected twelve of her students to reorganize the Christian Science Church in September, 1892, and they were known as "First Members." Two of those "First Members" were Mr. and Mrs. Ira Oscar Knapp. As an initial step in this undertaking, Mrs. Eddy made Mr. Knapp sole trustee of the land selected for the church building, and later made him one of four trustees, known as The Christian Science Board of Directors, entrusted to erect a church building on that land. She named Mr. Knapp chairman of the Board. Although deeply religious by nature, neither Mr. Knapp nor his wife ever joined a church, or any other organization, until they united with the Christian Science Church.

The story of The Mother Church could not be written without knowing the characteristics of some of the chief actors in that important enterprise. Ira Oscar Knapp was born in Lyman, New Hampshire, June 7, 1839, the son of Jehial and Daphne Bartlett Knapp. His ancestors were of the sturdy yeomanry, with marked moral and religious characteristics; and of the scores of relatives, not a dissipated nor an immoral person was known among them. His line of descent is traced from the Puritans through Aaron Knapp, who is said to have come from England with the early Plymouth colonists, and to have settled at Taunton, Massachusetts, about the year 1639. The Knapp coat of arms is recorded in heraldry as belonging to an English family of marked distinction.

Ira Knapp attended Peacham and Newbury Academies, and became a school teacher. Later, he became a prosperous farmer and increased his capital by successful business transactions. Turning to politics, he held at various times practically every office in the gift of the town, and finally became superintendent of schools. It was while serving as superintendent that he engaged as one of his teachers Miss Flavia F. Stickney, daughter of Ethan F. Stickney, of Lyman, New Hampshire. She had prepared herself for teaching at Newbury Academy, in Vermont. They were married May 1, 1866, and reared a family of four children.

Mrs. Knapp's father was a successful farmer, and her grandfather, Lebbeus Hastings, was a drover. His business was to purchase livestock for the Boston market and drive them over the road all the way from the Canadian border. When the railroad was completed from Boston to Concord, New Hampshire, the livestock were shipped from Concord by train. Thus Lebbeus Hastings was a forerunner of the modern stockyard operators.

Mr. Knapp and his wife took an active interest in local church affairs. In those days, the people of that hill country discussed religion as naturally as politics whenever they met along the road or in the village store. There were two churches in Lyman, a Methodist and a Universalist church, but when it became apparent that the town was not large enough to support both of them, the townspeople agreed to a union meeting-house at which the Universalist and Methodist preachers alternated every six months. The ministers were frequently entertained in the Knapp home, and Mr. Knapp led the church choir. The loss of his only brother, whom he dearly loved, turned him to a deeper and more searching study of the Bible and of religious matters. Although he was more inclined toward Universalism than any other religion, and was a regular attendant at the Sunday services, he never joined the church. His early experiences in business, politics, and religion were only footsteps preparing Ira Knapp for the great work which he was to accomplish for the Cause of Christian Science.

Christian Science was first brought to the attention of the Knapp family by Mrs. Knapp's sister, who lived in the adjoining town of Littleton. She reported some remarkable cases of healing by a Christian Science practitioner, Miss Julia S. Bartlett, and urged her sister to have some treatments. For thirteen years Mrs. Knapp had been suffering from ill health, and the physicians had pronounced her incurable. Her son, Ralph, had also developed a supposedly incurable trouble, and the futility of medical remedies had made Mr. and Mrs. Knapp so skeptical that, when urged to try Christian Science, Mr. Knapp remarked laconically, "Well, we will try one more humbug."

It was in the summer of 1884 that Mr. Knapp went to Littleton to see Miss Bartlett in regard to treatment. She was just returning to Boston, and could not take any more patients at that time. Mr. Knapp then wrote directly to Mrs. Eddy, and asked her to take his wife's case and his own, for he was suffering from some slight indisposition. Mrs. Eddy sent the letter by Calvin A. Frye to Mrs. Mary E. Harris in Boston, with the request that she should take these cases and answer the letter. Mrs. Harris, who later became Mrs. Curtis, was very glad to do this, and she began work at once, writing Mr. Knapp to this effect. In a week's time, Mr. Knapp wrote her that both he and his wife were much worse, and she could stop treatment. Mrs. Harris said that she knew perfectly well that this was only the effect of truth stirring up the error, and she went right on treating them. She treated them as God's spiritual children, not attacking the error this time, and she soon received another letter from Mr. Knapp, stating that he and his wife were much better, and asking her to continue the treatment. Mr. Knapp was quickly healed, and his wife was much improved.

Mrs. Knapp urged Mrs. Harris to come to Lyman for a visit, and she consented. When she left the train at Lisbon, she asked the station agent if Mrs. Ira Knapp had come to meet her. He looked up in amazement, and said, "Mrs. Knapp will never come to this station again." So Mrs. Harris got a carriage at the hotel, and just as she was starting for Lyman, a handsome, fresh-faced, young woman came up the steps of the hotel, and asked, "Have you seen a Mrs. Harris here?" Mrs. Harris immediately replied, "That is my name. Are you Mrs. Knapp's daughter?" and she was surprised at the response: "No, I am Mrs. Knapp, and I have my buggy right here to drive you to Lyman."

Mrs. Harris remained at the farm four days, and during that time she treated Ralph Knapp, who was quickly healed. Mr. and Mrs. Knapp drank in eagerly the truths of Christian Science which their guest shared with them, and they sent for the textbook, "Science and Health with Key to the Scriptures," by Mary Baker Eddy. After Mr. Knapp had gained some idea of the meaning of Christian Science, he exclaimed, "I have introduced physiology into these schools, and now I wish I hadn't!" Mrs. Harris reassured him by saying, "Don't let that trouble you. You did the best you knew at the time." After her visit, Mrs. Harris went to Lisbon for a few days, and there she had many wonderful cases of healing, most of them instantaneous.

Mrs. Knapp was completely healed in three weeks' time. As she gained her health and strength, she began to do many things she had not been able to do for years. The first time she walked to the home of her nearest neighbor, about a quarter of a mile away, the children all went too, dancing joyously around her.

After Mrs. Knapp's healing, the study of Christian Science was begun in earnest, and a new life opened for the whole family. Mr. Knapp spent most of his time with Science and Health and the Bible, literally wearing out the big family Bible and a copy of the textbook. He continued to superintend the farm work, but left most of the labor to others. During the summer months, he could be seen day after day sitting under a great butternut tree, poring over his books. Gradually he gave up all interest in town affairs. This change brought forth many unkind remarks from his friends and neighbors, who thought he had gone crazy on the subject of religion.

The following December, Mrs. Eddy called Mr. and Mrs. Knapp to take class instruction with her. The class opened the last week in December, 1884, and continued for three weeks. There was little time between the notice and the date set for the class. A telegram was sent from Boston on December 16, stating that the first session of the class would be held on December 22. It never occurred to Mr. and Mrs. Knapp that they could not accept, or that they could not make arrangements in time. Mrs. Knapp's aunt came and kept house for the family, and every need was quickly supplied.

It is truly remarkable how Mrs. Eddy, during three weeks' instruction in Christian Science, could completely transform a student's outlook on life. Her teaching not only changed Mr. and Mrs. Knapp's viewpoint, but lifted them entirely out of their former environment. Mrs. Knapp referred in a letter to the very searching nature of Mrs. Eddy's instruction. She spoke of the thought of the students as having been thoroughly plowed and harrowed to receive the seeds of truth.

Mrs. Eddy possessed the ability to read unspoken thoughts. For example: Mrs. Helen A. Nixon called at her home for an interview, and was told that Mrs. Eddy would see her in a few moments. While Mrs. Nixon waited for Mrs. Eddy, she saw an intoxicated man across the street. She began to ponder the case, and asked herself, "Where is that seeming error? Is the error in me or is it in him? Am I drunk or is that man drunk?" Immediately Mrs. Eddy, who had entered the room unobserved, said aloud, "No, that error is not in your thought." She had read the mental query and gave the answer to it before the student was aware of her presence.

One day during class, Mrs. Eddy asked every student to find a patient and report the next day the healing of the patient. Now, most of those pupils were strangers in the city, and their chief difficulty was to find a patient. Mr. Knapp mentioned his perplexity to his landlady, and she said at once, "You can heal me, for I am totally deaf in one ear." In his joy at having found a patient, Mr. Knapp rushed up to his room, and in a burst of spiritual illumination, he exclaimed, "In all the realm of the real, there is no such thing as deafness!" The woman immediately ran upstairs after him, declaring, "I am healed, I am healed!" She said there was a report like a pistol shot in her ear, and her healing was instantaneous.

When Mrs. Eddy asked the class to bring in cases of healing, Mrs. Knapp remarked, "Oh, I am not good enough to do that." After Mrs. Knapp returned to the lodging-house that day, she was passing along the hall when she heard someone groaning. She entered the room, and found a woman who had been suffering severely for some time. The woman welcomed any help Mrs. Knapp could give her; and in one treatment the patient was healed. Next day, when Mrs. Knapp was telling in class of this healing, Mrs. Eddy commented, "And you are the little woman who said you were not good enough to do that!''

Another case of healing is given by Mrs. Eddy as follows:

''Also, Mr. C. M. H___, of Boston, formerly partner of George T. Brown, pharmacist, No. 5 Beacon St., will tell you that he was my student in December, 1884; and that before leaving the class he took a patient thoroughly addicted to the use of opium — if she went without it twenty-four hours she would have delirium — and in forty-eight hours cured her perfectly of this habit, with no bad results, but with decided improvement in health.'' (Miscellaneous Writings, p. 242).

The spirit of this Christian healing with which Mrs. Eddy had blessed Mr. and Mrs. Knapp never left them. They returned to their home, and began to heal their neighbors. Those who came gladly were quickly healed; but as the scribes and Pharisees opposed the truth in the days of Jesus, so the same opposition to the healing Christ began to manifest itelf. It required courage to voice Christian Science in those days. Lifelong friends refused to speak to Mr. and Mrs. Knapp, and error became rampant in the effort to destroy, if possible, this Christ-healing.

After he returned from class, Mr. Knapp began to talk Christian Science to the minister then resident in Lyman. He showed great interest in the subject, and even read

Science and Health. Then he went to a Methodist camp meeting, and came back hostile to Christian Science. The following Sunday he read a sermon, probably written by someone else, denouncing Christian Science. Daphne Knapp, who was attending church with her father, noticed that he was greatly agitated, and she began to fear what might happen. At the conclusion of the sermon, Ira Knapp rose in his pew and asked permission to reply to the attack on Christian Science. His request was granted, and in a speech tense with restrained feeling, which electrified the staid congregation, he answered the preacher, point by point; and then sat down. The minister replied to him, and immediately announced the closing hymn. Mr. Knapp was not, however, to be put off so easily; he followed the minister into his Sunday School class, where he continued the discussion until he had silenced the opposition. Although he never again entered that church, Mr. Knapp was told that the next Sunday the minister apologized to the congregation for his attack on Christian Science, and said that he did not blame Mr. Knapp for replying to him.

After the incident in church, further opposition to Christian Science developed, until Mr. Knapp was notified that unless he gave up this new doctrine, he would be tarred and feathered and ridden out of town on a rail. Truth protected him in his work, however; but the patients were becoming intimidated; so he and his wife found it wiser to visit them only after dark and by the back doors.

Mrs. Eddy's rebuke to a student during Mr. and Mrs. Knapp's first class with her, was of great help to them. The classmate in question seemed to grasp the spiritual sense of Mrs. Eddy's teachings, without properly recognizing their application. He was continually making absolute statements of Christian Science, and ignoring the human footsteps. Finally, Mrs. Eddy stamped her foot, and calling him sharply by name, said, "Come down. Your head is way up there in the stars, while the enemy is filling your body with bullets." St. Paul showed the same practical wisdom when he said, "I keep under my body, and bring it into subjection: lest that by any means, when I have preached to others, I myself should be a castaway." Mr. and Mrs. Knapp gained from their class instruction a proper estimate of the human footsteps in Christian Science practice. They saw that above all, the absolute Science must be made practical, not only in healing work, but in daily living as well. And so they began to entrench themselves in Christian Science by demonstrating its teachings in their daily lives.

An interesting letter which Mr. Knapp wrote to Mrs. Eddy, describing an experience which came to him when he first accepted Christian Science, she had published in

The Christian Science Journal for April, 1888. During this experience, as he thought on the mission of Christian Science, he exclaimed, "It brings a message of Love," and then, to quote the exact words of his letter:

"To my surprise a voice — nothing like a human voice — answered and said: 'Where shall I abide? Your house is occupied. Turn out your old tenants, and put on one measure of humility, and another measure, and yet another measure; and then I will abide with you, and Charity will abide with you.'

"I pondered this a few days, and applied to you for instruction. Early one morning I was again surprised, with what seemed a mighty rushing wind, which no man could stay. It made the earth as a desert, and left me bare and naked; but before me was a great rock, square and upright; and on its sides the word Truth appeared. On this rock I saw that I must build.

"Now for over three years I have been trying to heed the voice of Truth, as taught by you in Christian Science; for I know 'it is the only way given under Heaven' that will enable us to stand with the Lamb on Mount Zion, to be numbered with the pure conceptions (virgins) which follow the Lamb whithersoever he goeth."(Vol. VI, p. 26).

All these early experiences in Christian Science were preparing Ira Knapp for his later work. His ability to heal the sick, his practical application of the teachings of

Christian Science to everyday problems, and his keen detection of any attempt to falsify Christian Science made him of great value to Mrs. Eddy in the activities of the Church. His earnest study of the Bible, even before he found Christian Science, was a preparation for his work on the Bible Lesson Committee.

The fact that Mrs. Eddy appreciated Mr. and Mrs. Knapp's sincerity and consecration to Christian Science, even in the early days, is shown in the following letter written to them by Mr. Frye shortly after their first class with Mrs. Eddy:

> "571 Columbus Avenue,
> Boston, Mass.
> May 9, 1885

"Mr. Knapp,
Dear Brother:

"Your letter of the seventh inst. to Mrs. Eddy received. Persons with such sincere motives and pure desires to honor God and do good, as you and your wife entertain, cannot fail of receiving the promise of the Master, 'Thou hast been faithful over a few things, I will make thee ruler over many,' etc. The effort to prevent the good results of your labors must be the work of other minds over which you have got to learn your way, or rather gain a realizing and abiding sense that *God is all*, and rebuke the false claim that *any mortal mind* can hinder you in your work.

"Mrs. Eddy wishes to be remembered to you and Mrs. Knapp and says that she will take you and your wife through another class. . . . There is no time appointed for next class, but it may not be until September.

Yours fraternally,

CALVIN A. FRYE"

II

TWO VISITORS TO THE KNAPP FARM

CHAPTER II

———————————— * ————————————

Two Visitors to the Knapp Farm

AFTER Mr. Knapp had accepted Christian Science, and had taken class instruction with Mrs. Eddy, the unfolding of truth in his consciousness was at times like a burst of revelation, and his spiritual perception became very keen. The book of Revelation, particularly, was illumined to him. He saw that its prophecies were applicable to the coming of Christian Science in this age, and he became so familiar with those prophecies that he was called by many Christian Scientists "the Revelation man."

Soon after his first class with Mrs. Eddy, at a time when he seemed to be lifted into the very heaven of Spirit, there came to Mr. Knapp a mental picture of the errors in mortal mind. When Daniel had his vision of the four Beasts, which symbolized the sum total of human sin, it made him sick. And this uncovering of sin that came to Mr. Knapp, frightened him so much that he wanted to run away, even as Moses ran from the serpent. But God commanded Moses to handle the serpent; so Mr. Knapp was likewise commanded to face that error and get the

mastery over it.   Obediently, though with fear and trem-
bling, he began to handle the serpent of material sense
with Christian Science, and great peace rested upon him.

Mr. Knapp's familiarity with the book of Revelation, and
the new light thrown upon it by the teachings of Science
and Health, enabled him to see the infinite distance that
lay between the God-crowned Woman of the Apocalypse
and the Babylonish woman.   No sooner had that clarifi-
cation been made, than he was put to a severe testing of
his convictions in a very subtle way.

One of Mrs. Eddy's students, who sat in the same class
with him, asked if she might visit Mr. and Mrs. Knapp
in their New Hampshire home.   This classmate, Mrs.
Josephine C. Woodbury, was eagerly welcomed.   Soon
she expressed the desire to give a talk on Christian Science
at the Lisbon town hall, and Mr. Knapp gladly arranged
the meeting for her.   However, her public talk and her
private conversations did not ring true to Mr. Knapp's
concept of Christian Science.   They reminded him of the
account in the book of Revelation of the Babylonish
woman, and his suspicions were so aroused that he wrote
to Mrs. Eddy about it.

Mrs. Eddy's response was immediate.   She sent for
Mr. Knapp to come to Boston at once.   That resulted in
the complete exposure of Mrs. Woodbury's error, and her
recall to Boston by Mrs. Eddy. Thereupon, Mrs. Wood-

bury turned her hatred on Mr. and Mrs. Knapp, and she also tried in many ways to harm the Cause of Christian Science, finally bringing a lawsuit against Mrs. Eddy. A letter which Mr. Knapp wrote to Mrs. Eddy in regard to this subject, Mrs. Eddy had published in *The Christian Science Journal* (Vol. VI, p. 409), under the caption, "The Scarlet Woman."

At the time he was called to Boston to expose the Woodbury error, Mr. Knapp spent the night in Mrs. Eddy's home at 385 Commonwealth Avenue. While awake in the night, he saw this vision: there appeared a beautiful white lamb surrounded by light. He could see it whether his eyes were closed or open. It remained before him for some time, and he was so joyous in beholding it, that he roused his bed-fellow, Dr. E. J. Foster, to see it. But this man (who became Mrs. Eddy's adopted son in November, 1888) could not see the vision at all. Three times the lamb appeared, and the third time an eagle also appeared, ready to swoop down upon the lamb. Mr. Knapp was filled with fear that the lamb might be destroyed, but it was not; the eagle could not touch the lamb. Soon the vision disappeared, never to return. Next morning, Mrs. Eddy explained the significance of the vision, and set Mr. Knapp's thought at rest.

In the summer of 1888, after Mr. and Mrs. Knapp had been practising Christian Science for nearly four years,

Mrs. Eddy visited them at their home in Lyman. A few weeks before, on June 12, while Mrs. Eddy was in Chicago, thirty-six of her students in Boston had turned traitor to the movement, and had stolen the Association books and placed them in the hands of a lawyer. When she learned of this disloyalty, Mrs. Eddy prayed earnestly for God to raise up some dependable workers to help her in carrying on her great Cause. As a result of this prayer, she was led to go for a quiet time to the White Mountain House in New Hampshire, which was owned and operated by Christian Scientists. She took with her on this trip Miss Anna Osgood, Dr. E. J. Foster, and Calvin Frye.

Mrs. Eddy decided that she would preach on Sunday, and she prayed to be shown where the service should be held. The answer came, "To the Jew first, and also to the Gentile." So it was arranged that she should speak in the parlor of the Fabyan House, where Jewish guests predominated. Lyman is about thirty miles south of the hotel in the White Mountains where Mrs. Eddy was staying, and when Mr. and Mrs. Knapp heard of her intention to preach that Sunday, they took their daughter, Daphne, and went to the service.

Only a few had gathered to hear Mrs. Eddy, mostly people from neighboring towns who already knew of Christian Science. Daphne Knapp said in later years that she could not remember the sermon, but she would never forget the beautiful way in which Mrs. Eddy read the Ninety-first Psalm, for it was the most inspiring experience she had known. After the meeting, Mrs. Eddy mingled with the guests, and enjoyed the view of Mt. Washington.

When they returned to the White Mountain House after the service, Mrs. Knapp went up to Mrs. Eddy's room to visit with her. Mrs. Knapp saw that her teacher did not seem happy in her surroundings. Dr. Foster had written to Mr. Knapp on July 18, 1888, as follows: "Mother said something about going to your house a few days then, but she did not authorize me to say anything about it, and perhaps it was only a passing thought." So Mrs. Knapp invited Mrs. Eddy to spend a few days at their farm. Mrs. Eddy replied that if Mr. Knapp would meet her the next day at the station in Lisbon, she would then decide according to God's guidance whether she would make the visit or not.

A short time before this, Mr. and Mrs. Knapp had made plans to go to Roslindale, a suburb of Boston, to look at a house which they had been urged to buy. So the morning after Mrs. Eddy had preached at the Fabyan House, they went to Lisbon to meet her, prepared to join Mrs. Eddy on the trip to Boston or to take her home with them, as God should direct. When the train reached the station, they found much to their joy that Mrs. Eddy had decided to go to Lyman. As she got off the train, she stood for a moment looking around her, and then remarked, "What a narrow little town!" Only a short while before, some of the leading citizens had hanged an effigy of Mrs. Eddy in the town square; and in the "horrible procession" on the previous Fourth of July, Mrs. Eddy had been caricatured as an insane woman in a cage, to whom a man, representing a local Scientist, was feeding medicine through the bars of the cage. These demonstrations showed how much the community was aroused against Christian Science because of the healings that had been accomplished there.

Mr. Knapp had two carriages waiting for the train. Mrs. Knapp drove Mrs. Eddy to the farm, while the other carriage accommodated the rest of the party except Miss Osgood, who continued her journey to her home in Vermont. The drive was over a quiet country road, up hill most of the distance of four and a half miles. The views of the surrounding mountains brought a restful sense to Mrs. Eddy.

The household consisted at that time of Mr. and Mrs. Knapp, their four children, a neighbor's daughter who helped with the housework during the summer, and a faithful farm hand who later became interested in Christian Science. Daphne Knapp, a girl scarcely eighteen years old, felt keenly her responsibility as the housekeeper and cook, and took pride in preparing a good dinner for Mrs. Eddy and her friends, who arrived at the house about eleven o'clock in the morning. It was an old-fashioned country dwelling, with a large square room on either side of the front door. One of these rooms, Mr. and Mrs. Knapp's chamber, which was on the northeast corner of the house, was assigned to Mrs. Eddy. It was a great event in this country home to have such distinguished guests, and everything possible was done for their comfort.

While Mrs. Eddy was visiting in the parlor, the youngest son, Bliss, introduced himself in an unusual way. He was a very shy lad, seldom presenting himself when there was company in the house, and this early appearance quite surprised the family. The little fellow went straight to Mrs. Eddy, and put into her lap a tiny yellow chicken. He said nothing, but remained standing by her while she talked to him about his pets. Taking the chicken out, he soon returned with a little kitten, which he also deposited in Mrs. Eddy's lap. Again she talked to him about his pets, and he soon took the kitten away. The introduction was over, and there was no more shyness during Mrs. Eddy's visit. She seemed never to have forgotten this incident, and in later years used to tell about it, even recalling it in a letter to the boy when he had become a man.

About the time that Mrs. Eddy started for the White Mountains, Ira Knapp began to have a most unusual experience. As he would sit with his books on a large rock under the shade of a great, spreading butternut tree, the vision of a brilliantly lighted city street kept presenting itself. It was always the same street, and he saw this vision very clearly in the daytime, when he was wide awake. He told Mrs. Eddy of this experience soon after her arrival, and he incidentally told her of the proposed trip to Boston to inspect the house in Roslindale. When Mrs. Eddy heard about the vision, she was deeply interested and said, "I understand;" and she insisted that both Mr. and Mrs. Knapp should take the trip to Boston as they had planned. They declared that nothing would induce them to leave such a loved and honored guest, until Mrs. Eddy told them that she would not stay unless they went to Boston; but if they did go, she would remain until their return. So the next morning they started for Boston, and were away three days.

After Mr. and Mrs. Knapp had gone in obedience to Mrs. Eddy's request, Daphne was left in charge of the guests. That first evening, Mrs. Eddy asked the whole household to come into the parlor, where she entertained them with stories of her childhood. She told the children about her grandmother's knitting; how she loved to sit on a little stool and watch her grandmother knit and keep time with her mouth to the needles. Mrs. Eddy showed them just how her grandmother held the needles in a shield pinned to her side, and went through the pretense of knitting and doing as her grandmother had done. She looked just like an old lady who had lost her teeth, as she worked her mouth to the tune of the needles. This recital amused them all greatly and they laughed heartily.

One day while Mr. and Mrs. Knapp were away, Mrs. Eddy took a walk, accompanied by Mr. Frye and Dr. Foster. They went to the top of a nearby hill commanding a grand view of the surrounding mountains and country-side, with many farms and thick woods in the distance, and a little lake in the valley below. Mrs. Eddy always had her meals with the family, and she showed a keen interest in all the work of the farm and household. One morning she watched the process of churning, working, and packing the butter, and sometimes she visited the kitchen. She did not say much on these occasions, but seemed to be a close observer.

After Mr. and Mrs. Knapp had returned, an incident which seemed to interest Mrs. Eddy occurred one day during the noonday meal. The door from the sitting room opened without ceremony, and in came a woman of about sixty years of age, typical of the country folk of pioneer days. She wore a full-skirted calico dress and a starched sunbonnet. Her face told of hard work and showed that she was unschooled, but nevertheless it was a kind and good face. She had come up for an afternoon visit, and, as she entered the room, greeted the family with the words, "How-de-do, folks." Mrs. Knapp took her to the kitchen to visit with the maid until after dinner. As soon as Mrs. Eddy had finished, she made some excuse to go to the kitchen, and as she went through the room and back again, she watched the woman who sat by the window, knitting. Mrs. Knapp supposed that the woman may have recalled some early memories; but the incident showed Mrs. Eddy's keen interest in different types of humanity.

One morning during Mrs. Eddy's visit, she was not ready at the usual time for breakfast. When Mrs. Knapp went to her room, Mrs. Eddy said that she had spent the whole night in prayer over some problem, and the outlook seemed dark and depressing. While Mrs. Knapp was talking with her guest, Daphne sat down at the organ and began to play and sing some Gospel hymns. The men joined in singing the old hymn, "Joy cometh in the morning." As Mrs. Eddy heard this dear old song and caught the words, she paused and listened, and her face brightened. When they had finished, she said to Mrs. Knapp, "Go and ask them to sing it again." This they gladly did, and sang it with even more spirit than at first. Then Mrs. Eddy arose, dressed herself, and soon came out to breakfast, radiant and happy. That little touch of His presence had scattered the clouds because she was *listening,* and immediately heard His message through the song.

Some years later, when Mrs. Eddy learned that Mr. Knapp was going through a period of stress, she wrote to him, reminding him of this incident in her visit, and advising him to turn to the same hymn for help. She wrote, "Sing again the old sacred song referred to on the first page of this letter — and sing it in the same spirit you had in New Hampshire when you sang it *years ago*." Ever since that time, this hymn has been an inspiration to the members of the Knapp family.

Mrs. Eddy came to visit Mr. and Mrs. Knapp on August 20, and left them the sixth day after dinner. As she was leaving, and was about to step into the carriage, Mrs. Eddy looked all around her and then at the four children, as though in deep thought. After she was seated in the carriage with Mrs. Knapp, she said, "I have taken all your children with me into Mind." The remembrance of these words was always a benediction to Mr. and Mrs. Knapp and their children.

Mrs. Eddy's next visit to the Knapp family was in their Roslindale home; for within the next two weeks, their farm had been exchanged for the house in Roslindale, and they had moved to Boston. The father of one of their neighbors in Lyman owned the house, and wanted to exchange it for Mr. Knapp's farm, so that he could live near his daughter. Although Mr. Knapp had been a trader all his life, he often said afterwards that *he* had nothing to do with this trade, — that God did it. The sale of the stock, crops, and tools was made in a most remarkable way, as though by prearrangement, and without any discussion. Whatever price was named by either party was accepted by the other, and in this way the farm and all its equipment were sold. Even some of the furniture was exchanged on that first visit to Roslindale.

It was on a Saturday evening that Mr. Knapp arrived at the North Station in Boston on his way to his new home. As he walked across Boston Common to the old Providence Station in Park Square to take the train for Roslindale, he reached an elevation from which he could look down Columbus Avenue. The street lamps had just been lighted, and there before him, Ira Knapp recognized unmistakably the street of his vision. It was on this street that Mrs. Eddy's Metaphysical College was located, and on this same street Mr. Knapp was soon occupying his first office for Christian Science practice.

After Mr. Knapp had settled in Roslindale, his chief concern was to get established again as a practitioner of Christian Science. One day, he took Science and Health under his arm, and started out to find someone who would listen to what he had to say about this Science, because he must talk to someone. He found one man who was somewhat receptive, but he returned home feeling that he had not accomplished much. About that time, Mrs. Eddy asked him to share an office with her student, Mrs. Mary W. Munroe, on Columbus Avenue. He was obedient, and went to his office daily for six weeks without having a single patient. Finally the opposition to his getting established as a practitioner gave way, and the patients began to come, and were healed. Their healing brought others, and soon he had a lucrative practice.

He continued to share the office with Mrs. Munroe for about seven years, until each bought a home in the Back Bay district of Boston. Mrs. Munroe was one of the original twelve "First Members" selected by Mrs. Eddy to reorganize The Mother Church, and she also served with Mr. Knapp on the Bible Lesson Committee.

Soon after Ira Knapp took the office on Columbus Avenue, Mrs. Eddy required all Christian Science practitioners to place their professional signs at the street entrance to their offices. But hardly any of the practitioners were permitted to do so, and a general search for new quarters began. The opposition to the name "Christian Science" was so great that the practitioners were reminded of Jesus' saying, "The Son of man hath not where to lay his head." Finally the mental opposition was overcome, and suitable offices were secured where the practitioners' signs could be displayed. Sometimes the signs were removed or stolen, but after a while the public got familiar with the name "Christian Science," and the active opposition disappeared.

It took great courage to raise one's voice for Christian

Science in those days. But the gallant stand made by those early workers, who proved that God would meet their every need, was an inspiration to others to press forward in the practical demonstration of Christian Science.

III

MRS. EDDY IN ROSLINDALE

CHAPTER III

———————————— * ————————————

Mrs. Eddy in Roslindale

MR. AND MRS. KNAPP had longed for the privilege of attending the Christian Science Church, and their move to Boston made this possible. The services were then held in Chickering Hall, on Tremont Street near West Street. The Sunday School convened at 1.45 P.M., and the church service was held at three o'clock. This arrangement made it possible for people of other denominations to attend Christian Science services in the afternoon. The congregation of about two hundred and fifty people came from a radius of over fifty miles from Boston. They were not fair weather attendants, but came rain or shine. Mr. Knapp and his sons used to walk a mile and a half to Forest Hills, where they took the horsecar into town, because the trains did not reach Boston in time for Sunday School. This was a two hours' journey!

Mr. Frank E. Mason was preaching when Mr. and Mrs. Knapp first attended church in Chickering Hall, but Rev. Lanson P. Norcross soon succeeded him. Occasionally, Mrs. Eddy herself preached the sermon, usually without previous announcement. A letter written by Mrs. Knapp to Mrs. William P. Dillingham, wife of the United States Senator from Vermont, gives an account of one of the services at which Mrs. Eddy preached. It was also the Sunday for admitting new members into the Church, and Mr. and Mrs. Knapp were among those whose names were read from the platform. The letter is in part as follows:

"Roslindale, Mass.

December 25, 1888

"My Dear Mrs. Dillingham:

"Last Sunday was a day never to be forgotten — words fail to give one a proper idea of it. The house was full, even the gallery, and I have been told that some could not get in. Our darling Teacher was perfectly lovely, and every one present must have felt a holy, uplifting sense and been benefited spiritually. The decorations of cedar and flowers around the pulpit were beautiful. . . .

"Fifty-two, I think, were taken into the Church, Mr. Knapp and I of that number. After the services, Mrs. Eddy went through the aisles, speaking to the people and talking with them. . . . Some came from Providence, Rhode Island, and some from Fall River, Massachusetts, and all around.

" . . . Ralph and Bliss each received a Christmas card from her (Mrs. Eddy) this morning, on the back of which is the Lord's Prayer and the Spiritual Version. . . .

"The Ninety-first Psalm is the subject for the next Friday evening meeting.

"Mr. Knapp's price for treatment is five dollars a week, the first in advance; and then he varies according to circumstances.

Yours with love,

F. S. KNAPP."

On September 1, 1889, the time of the church services was changed to 10.30 in the morning, the Sunday School convening at 12.00 o'clock. Nearly the entire congregation remained for Sunday School. After Calvin Frye had gone to Concord, New Hampshire, as Mrs. Eddy's secretary, his class of adults was given to Mr. Knapp, and it soon numbered over eighty. The International Bible Lessons were used in the Sunday School, as in other Protestant churches at that time. When later, the services were held in Copley Hall, Mrs. Knapp also had a class of adults, numbering nearly one hundred. Both Mr. and Mrs. Knapp continued teaching in Sunday School until adult classes were discontinued at the time that personal preaching was also abolished.

The members of those Sunday School classes used to ask some difficult questions, and Mr. Knapp's answer to one such question, printed in *The Christian Science Journal*, is typical of his ability along this line. The inquirer had asked the symbolic meaning of the cross and crown, and Mr. Knapp's reply is in part as follows:

"I think our cross is giving up all for God; putting resolutely aside these things that keep us from, or hinder our growth in, Truth. All the petty cares and vexations that come to us each day, must be nailed to the cross. Jesus tells us if we take up our cross and follow him, we are indeed his disciples; that is, we must take up this great claim of a 'mind of our own,' bear it patiently, and be constantly overcoming it by the power of Truth. The material crown, being a symbol of the highest earthly honor, is typical of what we may win — perfect spiritual rest and peace—by giving up all for Truth." (Vol. VIII, p. 497). Many cases of healing resulted from the truth brought out in these Sunday School classes.

About a year after Mr. Knapp had joined the Church, he was appointed by Mrs. Eddy to the important work of preparing Bible Lessons for Christian Science churches. Before this, in June, 1888, the following note was printed in *The Christian Science Journal:* "In the July number of our *Journal* . . . will appear Notes on the International Sunday-school Lessons, written from a Christian Science standpoint, by Frank E. Mason, C.S.B., assistant pastor of the Church of Christ (Scientist), Boston. These notes were issued at the request of our beloved Teacher and Pastor, Rev. M. B. G. Eddy. The object is to avoid conflict of ideas, and establish unity of thought." These lessons by Mr. Mason appeared in *The Christian Science Journal* from July, 1888, through November, 1889.

In an editorial in the December *Christian Science Journal*, 1889, it was announced that "Christian Science Bible Lessons" (International Series) were being prepared by a committee and would appear in January, 1890. This committee, which was appointed by Mrs. Eddy, consisted of Ira O. Knapp, Rev. Lanson P. Norcross, William B. Johnson, and Miss Julia S. Bartlett. Subsequently, the committee was increased to six members. At first the committee used the International Bible Lessons as a basis for their work, explaining the Bible texts by other Bible texts and by references from Science and Health. In July, 1898, the Lessons for the morning service began to appear in practically the same form as they now are, and on the same subjects selected by Mrs. Eddy that are still in use. The afternoon or evening service continued to follow the International Series. In April, 1900, the International Series was discarded entirely, and the second service became a repetition of the morning service.

The work of preparing these Lessons was a new and untried field of labor, and required much thought and prayer for spiritual guidance. The committee worked on the Lessons individually until a Lesson was in shape, and then examined it collectively. Mr. Knapp's four years of earnest study of the Bible and Science and Health in Lyman now bore fruitage; and without doubt the work on this Bible Lesson Committee aided him in his other activities as a pioneer in the Christian Science movement.

The first meetings of the Bible Lesson Committee were held in Miss Julia S. Bartlett's rooms in West Rutland Square, Boston. Later they were held in an unfurnished storeroom of The Christian Science Publishing Society, which was then located in the Hotel Boylston on the southeast corner of Boylston and Tremont Streets. Here the committee had for their use a rough table, with packing boxes for seats. When they began their work, there was no concordance to Science and Health, and in finding references, the committee had to depend upon their familiarity with the book. On one occasion, all the members of the committee agreed that a specific reference was needed, but no one seemed able to find it. At last one of them said, "Let us all open Science and Health and see if someone doesn't turn to the right place." This they did, and all except one opened directly to the reference in question.

About the time that the work of the Bible Lesson Committee was well started, Mrs. Eddy saw the need of moving away from Boston. So she left her home on Commonwealth Avenue, and rented a house at 62 North State Street, in Concord, New Hampshire. She needed more retirement to carry on her work for the Cause than she could find in Boston, but Concord seemed too far away from her church activities. So she asked Mr. Knapp to look for a home that would meet her needs. After a careful and prayerful search, he favored an estate in Roslindale. Mrs. Eddy had expressed a great desire to be near Mr. Knapp and his family; and when he had described the place in detail to her, she seemed to believe that it was the one "prepared for the Woman."

There was considerable interference in making a satisfactory trade. While these negotiations were going on, Mrs. Eddy wrote to Mr. Knapp, quoting the Psalmist, "It is 'very tempestuous round about Him' just now." It seemed easy for her to help others, but there was a struggle when she tried to accomplish something for herself. While reading the thirty-third chapter of Jeremiah, she felt that Love had made it clear that she could take the residence which Mr. Knapp had found for her.

The Roslindale estate was at that time the most beautiful and attractive in that locality. There were extensive gardens, a terraced lawn sloping to the street, and a stable and greenhouse in the rear. The property was purchased in the spring of 1891. Some alterations were made in the house; and Mrs. Eddy asked that a telephone connected with the telegraph office should be installed in Mr. Knapp's house for her convenience, as she did not wish a telephone in her own home. Loving hearts and hands arranged the furnishings in preparation for Mrs. Eddy's coming.

Shortly after Mrs. Eddy was settled, however, she discovered that her work was being interrupted in Roslindale just as much as it had been in Boston. And later, when she moved to Chestnut Hill, Massachusetts, she found the same conditions repeated, but in lesser degree, because the students had meanwhile been learning how to handle field problems.

In a letter to Judge Septimus J. Hanna Mrs. Eddy wrote:

"I possess a spiritual sense of what the malicious mental malpractitioner is mentally arguing which cannot be deceived. I can discern in the human mind, thoughts, motives, and purpose; and neither mental arguments nor psychic power can affect this spiritual insight. It is as impossible to prevent this native perception as to open the door of a room and then prevent a man who is not blind from looking into the room and seeing all it contains. This mind-reading is first sight; it is the gift of God. And this phenomenon appeared in my childhood; it is associated with my earliest memories, and has increased with years. It has enabled me to heal in a marvelous manner, to be just in judgment, to learn the divine Mind, — and it cannot be abused; no evil can be done by reason of it. If the human mind communicates with me in sleep, when I awake, this communication is as palpable as words audibly spoken." (Christian Science History by Septimus J. Hanna, First Edition, p. 16).

In "Miscellaneous Writings" Mrs. Eddy writes: "They who discern the face of the skies cannot always discern the mental signs of these times, and peer through the opaque error. Where my vision begins and is clear, theirs grows indistinct and ends." Then Mrs. Eddy proceeds to explain how one can recognize and act upon his God-given intuitions (p. 347).

Mrs. Eddy remained in Roslindale but a few months, and then returned to Concord, New Hampshire, and offered the Roslindale place for sale. During the brief time that Mrs. Eddy was Mr. Knapp's neighbor, occasionally he used to take her on her daily drive, and this gave her an opportunity to observe some of his characteristics. Although he had accepted Christian Science quite normally and had made it practical in daily experience, yet some of his views were rather extreme. For instance, after he came into Christian Science, he considered politics so corrupt and so unscientific that he refused to vote. This idea, however, was corrected when Mrs. Eddy showed him his duty as a good citizen. He also had an abnormal sense about celebrating birthdays. Mrs. Eddy saw that this, too, needed correction. So on his birthday, which

came during her stay in Roslindale, she sent him a present!
She gave him her photograph in a hand-painted frame
and a vase filled with beautiful flowers. She remembered
Bliss Knapp also on his birthday, by sending him her
favorite canary bird in a handsome brass cage. Mr.
Knapp learned his lesson, and from that time was less
extreme regarding ordinary human affairs. It must be
remembered, however, that any one who went to the
opposite extreme would also have merited Mrs. Eddy's
rebuke.

While she was still in Roslindale, Mrs. Eddy decided
one afternoon to call upon Mr. and Mrs. Knapp. She
walked through her garden gay with summer flowers, and
went across the street to their house. The family were all at
home, and were so glad to have the opportunity of thank-
ing Mrs. Eddy personally for various gifts which they had
received from her. Daphne Knapp was particularly ap-
preciative of her present — two charming black enameled
bracelets, which Mrs. Eddy herself had worn. Mrs. Eddy
observed, without comment, that Ralph Knapp was silent
amid all these expressions of gratitude, and she remembered that she had given him no present. Scarcely half
an hour after she had left the house, she sent Mr. Frye
over with a beautiful little clock for Ralph. This was but
one instance of Mrs. Eddy's loving consideration for all
with whom she came in contact.

After Mrs. Eddy's return to Concord, New Hampshire, Mr. Knapp was asked to search again for the home which Mrs. Eddy knew God had prepared for her. Early in December, 1891, she herself was led to a beautiful tract of land on the outskirts of Concord, which she purchased. She named her home "Pleasant View;" and in writing to Mr. Knapp about it, she said that she had longed for a home by the seaside, but instead God had prepared it on a hillside. She wrote, "My house here stands upon a very sightly hill, and the sides remind me of the Galilean slopes where my brother walked, and wept, and prayed."

IV

EARLY FOOTSTEPS IN CHURCH ORGANIZATION

CHAPTER IV

---✱---

Early Footsteps in Church Organization

SCIENCE AND HEALTH was written by Mrs. Eddy
as a scribe under orders from on high, and she became the closest student of what she had written. She
published the book in 1875; and in that same year, she
organized her students into the "Christian Scientist Association." Four years later this Association, on a motion
made by Mrs. Eddy, voted to organize a Christian Science
Church.

It is a matter of history that Jesus did not accept the
dogmas and traditions of the Jewish church. Referring
to that fact, Mrs. Eddy said, "He could not build his
(church) on their foundation; neither can we." (*The
Christian Science Journal*, Vol. VII, p. 13). She saw that
The Church of Christ, Scientist, must not only challenge
sin, as the Christian Church has always done, but it must
challenge also sickness and death, and thus restore the lost
element of Christian healing. Therefore, The Church of
Christ, Scientist, must be founded not on matter, but on
the complete revelation of Jesus Christ. To establish the

Church in this way required the same spiritual illumination which had enabled Mrs. Eddy to write Science and Health. She took the first steps in the organization of her Church, trusting God to open the way for further progress.

Twenty-six members of the Christian Scientist Association entered into an agreement to form a church, and at their first meeting for this purpose, held on April 12, 1879, they drew up the constitution of the Church, which was named the "Church of Christ, Scientist," in Boston. They recognized Mrs. Eddy as its Founder, and invited her to write the tenets and By-laws of the Church. In August of that year, 1879, a charter was secured, and Mrs. Eddy accepted the invitation to become the first Pastor of the Church of Christ, Scientist. She was duly ordained in 1881. The By-laws of the Church provided for a pastor, five directors, a treasurer, and a clerk, and stated that the pastor of this Church "must be able to heal the sick after the manner of Christian Science, must be strictly moral, and an earnest and devoted follower of Christ's Truth."

The infant Church prospered under Mrs. Eddy's preaching and guidance, and its growth made it desirable for the members to secure a church building of their own. In June, 1886, an agreement was made to purchase a church site, and a committee took the necessary steps to secure a lot in the Back Bay district of Boston, where the original edifice of The Mother Church now stands. The

treasurer of the Church secured the title to the lot by paying $2,000, and by giving a mortgage for the balance of
$4,800. The mortgage was to run for three years, or until
July 1, 1889.

After the land was purchased, means and methods for
raising money to pay off the mortgage in the allotted time
became the absorbing topic of interest to the members of
the Church. Now these former members of evangelical
churches had not been Christian Scientists long enough to
put off the old man with his deeds, for the new man
governed entirely by spiritual sense. They could not forget the old methods of raising money for church debts.
They thought of the church fairs, sociables, and suppers
they had been accustomed to, for they had not yet learned
that the spontaneity of unlimited supply is the normal fact,
which must be demonstrated by those who rely wholly
upon God.

The Sunday School girls in Mrs. Eastaman's class proposed the idea of holding a church fair to raise the necessary funds. The suggestion met with general approval;
but it was not in accordance with Mrs. Eddy's idea of
raising funds for The Church of Christ, Scientist, which
was breaking away from such traditional methods. It
seemed impossible, however, once the idea got under way,
to bring the church members to a more scientific sense of
the problem; for they would have the church fair.

It is scientifically certain that one's progress in Christian Science must come through Science or through suffering. If the church members were not sufficiently advanced to learn through the inspiration of Science, then they must learn through experience. Mrs. Eddy was, therefore, quick to waive her opposition when she saw the course they must take, and she gave her consent to the church fair. Committees were arranged for organizing and managing the fair, which was finally held on Monday, Tuesday, and Wednesday, December 19–21, 1887, in the old Horticultural Hall on Tremont Street at the corner of Bromfield Street. The hall was prettily decorated with fans, Japanese umbrellas, and embroideries. The eleven committees in charge provided for the refreshments, confectionery, flowers, needlework, and other commodities usually found at such bazaars.

After she had given her consent, Mrs. Eddy showed her magnanimity by coöperating to make the undertaking a complete success. She herself attended the fair on Tuesday evening to encourage the enterprise. As she was escorted from the door to the platform, the band played Mendelssohn's Wedding March. Her presence caused so much excitement, according to report, "as to impede the the wheels of gossip and barter." Mrs. Eddy spoke briefly of the Christian Science movement, and of the interest the children were taking in it. Her son and his children, who were visiting Mrs. Eddy at the time, also attended the fair.

Altogether the event was considered most successful. Nearly the whole amount necessary to cancel the mortgage had been raised, and it had all been done by the methods so familiar to those members who had but recently come out of the orthodox churches. They were to have a rude awakening, however; for in a short time the treasurer of the Church absconded with all the funds. Mrs. Eddy said of him after his disappearance, "He was an honest man:" and so he was by nature, and when left free from the evil influence that opposes the building of a church which is being established on a spiritual foundation. Alfred Lang was appointed treasurer of the Church Building Fund at the meeting held in February, 1889.

Long before the incident of the church fair, Mrs. Eddy had offered to purchase the site of a church building and to pay for it, but the members declined to accept such a gift from their Pastor. Now it seemed as if the Church would lose the lot and their first payment on it. Mrs. Eddy, however, quietly took the necessary steps to rescue the lot and to work out the problem according to Science. Six months before the mortgage note became due, she engaged a lawyer in Boston, Mr. Baxter E. Perry, to purchase the mortgage, which was done on December 4, 1888. Then Mrs. Eddy quietly waited. The date of the expiration of the mortgage, July 1, 1889, passed with no action

on the part of the Church.   One month later, Mrs. Eddy's
lawyer took the necessary foreclosure proceedings, and
advertised the lot for sale at public auction.   As no one
appeared on the day of the auction, August 3, Mr. Perry's
son, George, bid in the lot for $5,000 and took title to it on
August 6.   The mortgage was foreclosed the same day,
and the legal title was transferred from the Christian
Science Church to Mr. Perry's son.

Now that Mrs. Eddy had secured legal control of the
church lot, she intended to give all those Christian
Scientists, who were members of the Church when the lot
was originally purchased, an equal opportunity to secure
title to the lot at a private sale.   She intended, moreover,
if any Christian Scientist was alert enough to appear as a
purchaser, to pay for the lot herself and to donate it to the
Church, although no one but the purchaser was to know
that fact.   Certain days were designated for the sale, but
through some misunderstanding, it was advertised a day
late.   Meanwhile Mrs. Eddy handed a check for $5,100
to Mr. Knapp, with instructions to purchase the lot in his
own name, in case no other Scientist appeared.

Her instructions required Mr. Knapp to go to Mr.
Perry's office, present his practitioner's card bearing the
words, "Christian Scientist," and point out to Mr. Perry
his advertisement as a practitioner in *The Christian Science
Journal*.   Then Mr. Perry would sell him the lot.   The

opportunity provided for the church members to secure the lot was lost, however, through a mistake in sending Mr. Knapp to make the purchase a day earlier than was intended, and also because the lawyer had advertised the sale a day later than Mrs. Eddy had specified. She was therefore apprehensive that the students, because of this misunderstanding, might think that she was partial to Mr. Knapp. However, he arrived according to instructions, and Mr. Perry transferred the deed of the land to him on December 10, 1889. Mr. Knapp was well versed in writing deeds, and Mrs. Eddy left the wording of this one entirely to him. The messenger who handed him the check asked him not to cash it, but to hand it to Mr. Perry as it was, so that he in turn could give it back to Mrs. Eddy.

The title, freed from all encumbrances, was now legally held by Mr. Knapp. In less than a year after he had joined the Church, Mrs. Eddy had taken the first step in committing to him the great work for which he had been called from the New Hampshire hills.

Something very momentous was taking place in Mrs. Eddy's thought during the year 1889. She was impelled, as we have seen, to move from her Commonwealth Avenue home in Boston to Concord, New Hampshire. She realized that if the church members were to make progress, they must have the experience that positions of responsibility in the movement would involve, and thus allow her more freedom to work on the problem of establishing her Church.

Mrs. Eddy, therefore, withdrew as teacher of the Massachusetts Metaphysical College (*The Christian Science Journal*, Vol. VII, p. 204), and appointed Dr. Foster Eddy and Gen. Erastus N. Bates as teachers in her stead. She disorganized the College itself in September of that year. She found it impossible to attend the annual meeting of the National Christian Scientist Association, held that year in Cleveland, and resigned as its President; and she also resigned as Pastor of her Church. On December 2 of that same year, 1889, she caused the Church to disorganize, although neither the charter nor the name was surrendered; and the members continued to meet and hold services as a voluntary association. In *The Christian Science Journal* for December, 1889 (Vol. VII, p. 434; see also Miscellaneous Writings, p. 359), Mrs. Eddy wrote: "Material organization is requisite in the beginning; but when it has done its work, the purely Christly method of teaching and preaching must be adopted."

It is significant that this great forward movement in the development of the Church took place during the year following the desertion of the Cause by thirty-six of Mrs. Eddy's disloyal students. This purging of the ranks, which occurred in the summer of 1888, enabled Mrs. Eddy to lead her Church forward more rapidly. She was seeking in her retirement the opportunity to work out the details of a plan which was unfolding in her thought. It had been revealed to her clearly and definitely that a Christian Science Church, whose mission is to challenge sickness as well as sin, must partake of the Christly nature in order to make that challenge effectual. She also perceived that God's acres must not be held by a wholly material title. How to secure a title that should not be wholly material was the real problem before her, for Science must be "demonstrated by degrees." (*The Christian Science Journal*, Vol. VII, p. 434; see also Miscellaneous Writings, p. 359).

Having gone through the preliminary steps of making Mr. Knapp sole trustee of the church lot, and of causing the Church to disorganize, Mrs. Eddy was now ready to give a more spiritual title to the church property. There was a reason why the title should be held by a student rather than by herself. She still had some misgivings as to whether her students were sufficiently governed by the spirit of Christ to carry out her plan. With a desire to be rid of future care, in the event of their failure to follow her guidance, a failure which might lead to the breaking of the deed, she intimated that it would be well to have the title revert to a student rather than to herself. Of course this student must be one who had enough spiritual insight to accept her leadership and to coöperate with her implicitly. Evidently she realized, from what she knew of Mr. Knapp since his first class with her, and from the prophetic visions which he had related to her, that here was at least one of the disciples for whom she had prayed.

When Mr. Knapp first took class instruction in Christian Science, the chapter on the Apocalypse had not yet appeared in Science and Health; but Mrs. Eddy explained the twelfth chapter of Revelation to the class. Her explanation must have conveyed a profound meaning to those students, for although Mrs. Eddy made no reference to herself personally, Mr. Knapp exclaimed, "Thou art the Woman!" She turned to him and gave him a sweet smile, and did not rebuke him.

Said Mr. Knapp later, in explanation of his comment, "It must be apparent to the spiritualized consciousness of humanity, and to all loyal students of Christian Science, that Mary Baker Eddy is the human exponent of the two great wings of faith — Christianity and Science. This scientific Christianity she has expounded in 'Science and Health with Key to the Scriptures' — that leaf from the book of Life, which Christ Jesus has revealed as coming through the Woman in the Apocalypse. This Woman was destined to fulfill his revelation of Truth on earth as it is in heaven; for the bonds of earth are loosed in heaven. The recognition of the identity of this Woman in the Apocalypse is just as humanly and divinely essential to the followers of Christian Science today, as it was for the disciples of Jesus to acknowledge his living faith, as exhibited on earth over eighteen hundred years ago. To recognize the Christ of that day, enables one to recognize today the Science of Christianity, which heals the sick and preaches the everlasting gospel of peace from heaven. To know this Science unfolds the meaning of the signs of these times, and where we stand in relation to God and our fellow men. God's way of salvation is revealed, the signs of promise are appearing, and no other signs shall ever be given."

Although Ira Knapp's knowledge of human nature had taught him never to take any man's word for granted, all this was completely changed in regard to Mrs. Eddy as soon as he had recognized her place in Bible prophecy. He knew that she was God's messenger to this age, one of the two divinely appointed Witnesses. Then he could never question nor doubt any instruction or requirement which might come to him from God's Witness. In obeying her, he knew that he would be doing God's will, for Mrs. Eddy said as much to him in several letters which appear later in this book. When Peter awakened to behold and acknowledge his Master as the Christ, Jesus found in that acknowledgment the foundation for the Church of Christ. When Ira Knapp recognized his teacher as God's Witness, Mrs. Eddy found in that recognition a consciousness which could be helpful to her in building The First Church of Christ, Scientist. This acknowledgment in the hearts of Christian Scientists was the foundation upon which the Church must be built. Then the gates of hell could not prevail against it.

The next step in Mrs. Eddy's plan was for Mr. Knapp to convey the church lot to three trustees. A trust deed, which her New Hampshire lawyers had prepared, was handed to Mr. Knapp. He was asked to have it executed by Mrs. Eddy's lawyer in Boston, who had coöperated with her so fully up to this time. But hitherto this lawyer had been handling only ordinary points of law with which he was quite familiar. Now he was asked to execute a deed which seemed to him defective; in reality, he was asked to assist Mrs. Eddy in making her first move in establishing the spiritual structure of her Church. He refused to have anything to do with the transaction. Indeed, he would not even allow his name to appear on the deed as Justice of the Peace. For a lawyer of standing and ability thus to inveigh against the defects of a deed might have impressed some men and caused them to question the wisdom of its author. Not so with Mr. Knapp; he had learned that obedience to Mrs. Eddy was paramount, and even legal opinions could not outweigh the instructions from God's appointed messenger. Without any hesitation, he went immediately to another lawyer, who signed and executed the deed on December 18, 1889. This action of Mr. Knapp's proved to Mrs. Eddy that he could and would measure up to the spiritual requirements necessary to help her in building her Church.

Mrs. Eddy in her trust deed named five men as Directors of the Church, as follows: Ira O. Knapp, Joseph S. Eastaman, Eugene H. Greene, David Anthony, and William B. Johnson. The deed gave them the privilege of adding two more to their number and of filling vacancies on the Board. These Directors were to maintain Sunday services and procure a regular preacher for the Church. The deed also provided for a board of three trustees, whose business it was to hold in trust the title to the church lot, but *only* for the purpose of erecting a church edifice thereon. They must begin building operations only after the sum of $20,000 had been collected for that purpose, and the treasurer was to give a bond to the Trustees of $5,000 to insure the faithful discharge of his duties in office.

The deed further provided that none of the Trustees nor of the Directors should bring to Mrs. Eddy any matter of business relating to the fund or to the building of the church, under penalty of forfeiting his position. If any of the provisions of the deed were violated, the land would revert to Mr. Knapp or his heirs. An important point in the deed was the clause giving the Directors permission to organize the Church in the usual form at any time they desired. That point proved later to be the test of the Trustees' discipleship, when evil tempted them to wonder who would own God's temple.

When it became known that the building lot had been restored by Mrs. Eddy to the Church, in the form of a trust deed given to their Board of Directors, the members of the Church were very grateful, and expressed their gratitude in a letter to Mrs. Eddy. They acknowledged that, as the time approached for paying off the mortgage, they had not sufficient funds in the treasury to make the payment. Their humility and obedience in acknowledging their debt to Mrs. Eddy were gratifying. Their former unwillingness to have her own the land had now given place in God's own way to grateful acquiescence in her wishes.

The answer to Mrs. Eddy's own question as to whether she would give the lot to the Church, or to Christian Scientists in general, had also evolved satisfactorily. The first point was settled when she disorganized the Church; the second point was decided by giving the land to trustees, who should hold it for Christian Scientists in general. Thus the Church would not be local to Boston, nor to Massachusetts, nor would it be local in any sense whatsoever. The lot was given to trustees for a Christian Science church building, which should be The Mother Church for all mankind. According to the provisions of the deed, the Board of Trustees organized with the three members named in the deed, as follows: William G. Nixon, Marcellus Munroe, and Alfred Lang. The deed designated Mr. Munroe as secretary, and Mr. Lang as treasurer of the Board.

With the church lot free from debt and $500 in the treasury, the Christian Scientists seemed to take a new lease of life in planning to raise the first $20,000 necessary to start the building. After the Church was disorganized, greater unity of thought and an increased manifestation of brotherly love were evident among the members. A great outpouring of love was now shown by the contributions which flowed into the building fund. Individuals, Sunday School classes, and Associations vied with each other in adding to the fund; and, according to the requirement of the trust deed, a list of contributions was published semi-annually in *The Christian Science Journal*.

This great burst of enthusiasm on the part of the members developed, however, into two distinct phases of misguided zeal: the first covering a larger part of the year 1890, and the second extending through the year 1891. In *The Christian Science Journal* for February, 1890, one of the Directors, Mr. Eugene H. Greene, expressed the thought that it would be a fitting tribute to their Leader to make the new church a memorial to her. The proposal met with a hearty response, and was earnestly discussed for some months before it came to Mrs. Eddy's attention. As soon as she heard of it, she promptly voiced her objections. She showed the students that to build the church with this object would be to turn from Principle to personality, and would thus bring the Church back to a material basis. The lot had been donated to build a house for the worship of God; and His true followers should "worship Him in spirit and in truth."

The fact that the church members had been led off so readily on such a tangent, and made so soon to forget the true foundation of the Church, showed the need of a greater spiritual awakening and a deeper consecration to their sacred purpose. "For when the Gentiles, which have not the law, do by nature the things contained in the law, these, having not the law, are a law unto themselves." (Romans 2:14). So must the Scientists learn to be a law unto themselves.

In the spring of 1891, another Director, Joseph S. Eastaman, put forward the idea of including in the church building a home for all the Christian Science activities, so that the edifice would be a combination of church and publishing house. Others, including Dr. Foster Eddy, had urged this plan before, but it was rather astonishing for a Director to advocate it so strongly, since the trust deed itself definitely stated that the building to be erected on the church lot should be exclusively a church edifice.

To add a publishing house would, therefore, violate the deed itself and forfeit the land. This provision, however, seems to have been entirely overlooked; for early in the year, it was definitely determined that the building should include a Christian Science Publishing House.

One of the chief reasons urged for this plan was that a church edifice would appeal only to local contributors, whereas a publishing house would have a national appeal. The students had evidently lost the point of Mrs. Eddy's refutation of that very argument. As the words "Christian Science" are the greatest and most comprehensive in our language, so The Mother Church is more than an international Church — it is universal; and Mrs. Eddy has said, "The star of Bethlehem is the star of Boston." (Miscellaneous Writings, p. 320).

Plans went forward, however, for making contributions to the building fund; the members were urged to increase the sale of the new edition of Science and Health by purchasing it wholesale and selling it at retail, and thus earning money for the church. The National Christian Scientist Association decided to postpone its next annual meeting, and the members were invited to contribute the amount of their traveling expenses to the fund. A children's fund, later known as "The Busy Bees' Fund," was started by Miss Maurine Campbell, so that old and young were at work raising money to build the church.

Meantime, the Trustees were developing the plans for a church building which should include publishing rooms. Finally the requisite $20,000 had been collected, and a set of plans was published in *The Christian Science Journal* for March, 1892. But fear crept in, and it was agreed that it would be unwise to start building until $30,000 had been contributed. The thought was expressed, however, that by April 1, the $30,000 would surely be in hand, and that building operations could then begin.

V

OBSTACLES TO CHURCH BUILDING

CHAPTER V

———————*———————

Obstacles to Church Building

FOR about two years, the Christian Scientists proceeded in unity and prosperity to carry out their purpose of raising the amount necessary to start the church edifice. During this time, the Trustees had sent out two circular letters asking for funds to erect a church building which should include publishing rooms: the first, about May 25, 1891; and the second, about February 15, 1892. These letters met with an immediate response, so that the Scientists were confident that by April 1, 1892, they could actually start the building of the church.

Just as these plans began to take definite form, the legality of the trust deed was questioned. For over two years, Mr. Nixon had believed that the title to the land given by Mr. Knapp to the Trustees was defective. He declared this to be his judgment as a business man with some knowledge of legal matters. Acting upon this belief, within two months after the deed was executed, he took a certified copy of the instrument to Mrs. Eddy, and pointed out to her what seemed to be the errors in the deed, and advised her to have them corrected.

Now it must be remembered that Mrs. Eddy was seeking to give a title to The Church of Christ, Scientist, which should not be wholly material. But the spiritual perception so necessary to the Trustees, in order to carry out the provisions of their trust, was overshadowed in Mr. Nixon's thought by what he considered important legal defects in the deed. Mrs. Eddy, doubtless, recognized this as part of the opposition to her advanced step in church building. The trust deed which she contemplated must be so framed as to test one's faith in her wisdom; and that element of faith would constitute its divine hue. She therefore endeavored to quiet Mr. Nixon's thought by assuring him that all imperfections would be corrected, and that he must have more faith to go on with the work.

There, apparently, the matter rested until the Trustees were actually ready to begin operations. Then Mr. Nixon again questioned the soundness of his trust, and on March 1, 1892, placed the deed in the hands of The Massachusetts Title Insurance Company for careful examination and report on the legal status of the title. That company reported that the deed was defective in four particulars, the chief of which concerned the ownership. First, the deed lacked the words of inheritance, "to their heirs," so that with the death of the last Trustee, the land

and the church building would revert to Mr. Knapp and his heirs. Second, in default of certain terms and conditions in the deed of conveyance, the land would revert to Mr. Knapp and his heirs. Third, since December 2, 1889, when the church organization was abandoned, there was no avowed membership which could hold property, and therefore the trust might be termed a "public charity," under the supervision of the Supreme Court. Fourth, Mr. Knapp's wife had not released her dower rights when the deed was granted.

From a legal point of view, all these arguments against the deed seemed to be valid. Indeed they seemed to be so reasonable and logical, that the Trustees were considerably irritated because Mrs. Eddy regarded these points as secondary to the spiritual problem of establishing and building her Church. The Trustees openly expressed their disregard for her by declaring some of the provisions of the deed to be purely "technical" and "frivolous."

Mrs. Eddy, however, recommended that the Trustees should consult with Mr. Perry, her attorney in Boston. His opinion was in agreement with that of The Massachusetts Title Insurance Company, and he told of his refusal to execute the deed, or to allow his name to appear on it as Justice of the Peace, when Mr. Knapp first handed it to him. Furthermore, he told the Trustees that this deed was the worst one he had ever seen, and that it courted expensive litigation and final loss of the property. These legal opinions tended to poison the thought of the Trustees more and more against Mrs. Eddy's main purpose, namely, to establish The First Church of Christ, Scientist, on a basis that should not be wholly material, and would therefore be endowed with the elements of eternity.

Mr. Perry was quite definite in his statement that the first step towards curing the title was for the Church to reorganize as a legal church body, in order to take title to the property. Mr. Knapp could then convey the land to an organized Church, instead of to trustees, and at the same time release his wife's dower. In a legal sense, this seemed to be a very simple and reasonable way out of the difficulty, especially since the terms of the trust specifically granted to the Directors the right to reorganize.

Armed with these legal opinions, the Trustees refused to proceed with building construction unless the defects of the deed should be remedied according to the lawyers' recommendations. Mrs. Eddy's hopes and expectations of an immediate start on the church edifice were consequently blocked, until some of these snarls could be untangled. The Trustees then brought pressure to bear on Mr. Knapp, as grantor of the trust and also as chairman of the Board of Directors, to consent to a reorganization of the Church. He, however, had deep respect for Mrs. Eddy's counsel. He realized that she was proceeding, not according to man's wisdom, but in obedience to that divine direction which would in time disclose the foolishness of the worldly wise. So he asked Mrs. Eddy for guidance. She promptly warned him not to follow the course recommended by the Trustees, and assured him that she would keep him advised as to what he should do.

There were some points about which Mrs. Eddy was definitely certain. In *The Christian Science Journal* (Vol. X, p. 133), she states that the "circuitous, novel way" by which she had given the land to the Church would in the end be found eminently wise. She also says in the same article: "I knew that to God's gift, foundation and superstructure, no one could hold a wholly material title. The land, and the church standing on it, must be conveyed through a type representing the true nature of the gift; a type morally and spiritually inalienable, but materially questionable — even after the manner that all spiritual good comes to Christian Scientists, to the end of taxing their faith in God, and their adherence to the superiority of the claims of Spirit over matter or merely legal titles. No one could buy, sell, or mortgage my gift as I had it conveyed." (See also Miscellaneous Writings, p. 140).

Apparently, any legal defects in the deed were considered by Mrs. Eddy as fitting opportunities for taxing the Christian Scientists' faith in God and in her leadership, and also for testing their fidelity to the claims of Spirit.

When Mr. Nixon first called her attention to these defects, she knew that if he only had enough faith to trust her guidance, the building could go on, and any legal defects could be remedied as the necessity might arise. Such obedience required more faith than Mr. Nixon could repose in Mrs. Eddy's leadership. Had he ever seen or acknowledged her as the Woman in the Apocalypse, he never could have doubted her wisdom and spiritual foresight.

Complete unity of thought had prevailed among the students from the time of the disorganization of the Church until the first of March, 1892, when the Trustees sought "to know who owned God's temple." (*The Christian Science Journal*, Vol. X, p. 134; see also Miscellaneous Writings, p. 140). Although Mrs. Eddy apparently realized that there were some legal defects in the title, she declared that "with the spirit of Christ actuating all the parties concerned about the legal quibble, it can easily be corrected to the satisfaction of all." (*The Christian Science Journal*, Vol. X, p. 135; Miscellaneous Writings, p. 141). To Mrs. Eddy, the paramount necessity was to start the church edifice in Boston with the resources at hand. Nothing was of the least concern compared with the supreme importance of commencing the erection of the church edifice. Mrs. Eddy realized that these legal controversies were avenues of evil to delay the building.

How few can perceive that when a thing seems to be materially right, it can be at the same time spiritually wrong! As Mrs. Eddy says in Science and Health (p. 491), there is "a negative right and a positive wrong." That which is positively right proves its righteousness by its allegiance to Christ. But so long as an error is challenged by a mentality on the same plane of belief as the error, there can be no progress. "As Moses lifted up the serpent in the wilderness, even so must the Son of man be lifted up;" and being lifted up in consciousness, he must in like manner lift thought to a spiritual sense of Church. Spiritual perception must outweigh material judgment. Hence Jesus' inditement of the lack of spiritual perception sometimes found in the legal profession: "Woe unto you, lawyers! for ye have taken away the key of knowledge: ye entered not in yourselves, and them that were entering in ye hindered." (Luke 11:52).

Mrs. Eddy found comfort, however, in the fact that Mr. Knapp could accept implicitly her point of view without being troubled over the legal quibble. She had another loyal supporter, also, on the Board of Directors in Mr. William B. Johnson. He, too, had that spiritual perception which outweighs merely material judgment, and this perception enabled him to help rather than to hinder Mrs. Eddy's work. At a church meeting called for the purpose of obtaining contributions to meet the increased expenses of the growing Church, Mr. Johnson had been tested as to his spiritual reliance on God as the source of supply. When the request was made for extra contributions, he had only five dollars in his pocket. It was a struggle for him to know whether he could trust God enough to give his last five dollars to the Church. By acting on impulse, he could easily do so and win the applause of his fellows; but unless he was guided by spiritual realization or demonstration, his action could be of no lasting benefit either to himself or to the Church. As he prayed over the matter, the realization of his true supply came to him, and with that realization came the faith to give his all.

Later in the day when Mr. Johnson returned home, he found two patients awaiting him, and each paid him five dollars in advance for a week's treatment. He afterwards said that, while he was struggling to know whether he could trust God to the extent of giving his last five dollars, those two people were doubtless struggling to know whether they could trust him for healing. When he established his own reliance on God, the question was settled for those two prospective patients. Moreover, such experiences taught him to understand and support Mrs. Eddy in her effort to establish her Church on a spiritual foundation.

In a confidential letter to Christian Scientists, dated

May 3, 1892, Mr. Johnson warned them of an evil influence that was endeavoring to make the Trustees say
that their deed was illegal, because it lacked the clause,
"to their heirs and assigns." He declared that one great
hindrance to starting the building was a plot for diverting
the use of the building fund to the erection of a rival church
on some other lot, which would be unrestricted. Although
the plot did not actually succeed in winning the Trustees,
as evil had done in the case of a former treasurer, it did
succeed in creating suspicion of the trust deed, and in
causing a demand for reorganizing the Church. The
church charter, be it remembered, had never been surrendered; and to reorganize the Church would have
enabled those malcontents, who had been eliminated by
the disorganization, to make trouble for the Church, if
indeed it would not actually have revived their membership.

These warnings of a plot were also voiced by the
Directors in a circular letter they addressed to the field on
June 7, 1892. In that circular, they quoted Mrs. Eddy's
comment on the possible necessity of returning the money
to the contributors as "terrible for our Cause but . . . of
the two evils, it is less than for your money to build a
church for the enemies of Christian Science, as no doubt
it will if left to the dictation of . . . error as at present."

The controversy over the title to the land went on between the Trustees and Mr. Knapp throughout the spring of 1892. There were two ways, as Mrs. Eddy saw it, by which victory could be gained: one, by "a material hard fought battle;" the other, in God's way. Mr. Knapp, acting entirely on advice from Mrs. Eddy, was endeavoring to bring about God's way. The Trustees, on the other hand, insisted upon the material law. Forbidden by the deed to consult Mrs. Eddy on the matter, the Trustees showed considerable bitterness towards Mr. Knapp, and by that means Mrs. Eddy could learn quite accurately their attitude towards her views.

Mrs. Eddy could lead the Church no faster than the Church as a whole could go. As we have already seen in the instance of the church fair, she allowed the members to learn, through suffering, lessons which they refused to learn through Science. This willingness to let God's way be worked out had given her the possession of the church lot, which was what God wanted her to have. Now, when the members, led by the Trustees and backed by legal counsel, demanded a reorganization of the Church for the purpose of taking legal title to the land, Mrs. Eddy finally addressed a letter to them dated May 10, 1892, giving her permission to reorganize. With the permission, however, went a warning to the members as to the consequences of such a step. If they reorganized, she declared that they were liable to lose: first, their present prosperity;

second, their form of government; third, the gift of land; for Mrs. Eddy knew only too well how the belligerent Scientists could take advantage of reorganization. Furthermore, in the face of all that had been said to the contrary, she maintained that it was still safe to build the church edifice on that land under the present trust deed.

The Trustees, however, continued to urge Mr. Knapp, as chairman of the Board of Directors, to call a meeting of the Church for the purpose of reorganizing. Although Mrs. Eddy instructed him in a letter dated May 11, 1892, to say no more against reorganization, and she herself would no longer oppose it, thus leaving the matter in the hands of God, nevertheless the Trustees could not gain Mr. Knapp's active coöperation in a proposition which he knew to be wrong. The church members also were beginning to awaken to the situation, and were unwilling to take the responsibility of bringing upon themselves the consequences stated in Mrs. Eddy's letter; and so they let the matter of reorganizing drop. At a meeting of the Christian Scientist Association held on June 1, 1892, it was unanimously voted that they should proceed at once to build the church and publishing rooms as the conditions then stood in relation to the title. But not until this action had been taken by the Association, were the Trustees definitely convinced, after nearly three months of effort, that there was no hope of gaining Mr. Knapp's consent to reorganize.

Meanwhile, Mr. Knapp was endeavoring under instructions from Mrs. Eddy to correct the defects in the deed, so that the building might go forward under a legal title.   On May 10, 1892, she wrote him as follows: "Go with witness to each Trustee and offer to make the deed legal if it is not already."   He was perfectly willing to remedy the defect in regard to his wife's inheritance.   He was also ready to insert the words, "heirs and assigns," to insure to the Trustees a continuance of their trust.   In the event of that change, Mrs. Eddy instructed him to say after the words, "heirs and assigns," that they must continue the building as a place for the "true worshippers in Christian Science."   But Mr. Knapp was not permitted by Mrs. Eddy to change the terms of the deed itself.   She insisted that the provision should remain in the deed that any breach of its requirements would cause the land to revert to him.

Mr. Knapp also presented to the Trustees a plan by which he agreed to give a bond to remedy the title to the deed, provided they would proceed to use the $30,000 in their hands for a church building.   The attorneys for the Trustees advised them not to consider this proposition for a moment, as it was wholly unwise; and the Trustees also claimed that they had no right to spend any money without fully informing the contributors of the conditions of the title, and gaining their consent to use the money for building.

Another circular was, therefore, sent out by the Trustees, dated June 13, 1892, explaining the condition and inclosing a blank on which the contributors were asked to state whether the Trustees should proceed with the building of the edifice as the title then stood. The Trustees agreed that they would go on with the construction of the building after $20,000 of the money then in their hands had been voted by the contributors to be used for that purpose. Should less than $20,000 be voted, the Trustees would refuse to begin operations. The blank sent out with this circular read as follows:

* . . . . *June* 1892

ALFRED LANG
MARCELLUS MUNROE } Trustees
W. G. NIXON

Gentlemen:

Having carefully read and considered your circular letter dated June 13, 1892, I hereby authorize and empower you to expend the sum of. . . . . . Dollars now in your hands and contributed by me, in erecting the proposed CHURCH OF CHRIST (Scientist) Boston, on

---

* Insert Town or City and Date
Have your signature witnessed.

the lot of land corner Falmouth and Caledonia Streets, deeded to you as Trustees, by Ira O. Knapp, on Dec. 17th, 1889.

.   .   .   .

Witness

.   .   .   .

If this blank is used return same by mail at once, to ALFRED LANG, Treasurer, 279 Broadway, Lawrence, Mass.

After this circular was issued, Mrs. Eddy wrote to Mr. Lang, the Treasurer, who was also the one designated to have charge of the building construction, entreating him either to use the money on hand to erect a church edifice, or to return the contributions to the donors. The Trustees' reply indicated that they had practically agreed sometime before to take the latter course; and as a matter of fact, by August 29, 1892, they had been requested by the contributors to return $22,000 of the money which had been collected.

Meanwhile, the tables were turned by the appearance of a circular letter from the Board of Directors, dated June 7, 1892, explaining to the field Mrs. Eddy's attitude on some of these points. This circular declared in no uncertain terms that if Mr. Nixon actually knew, as he claimed he did, that the deed was imperfect from the first, then the Trustees had no legal right to collect money for building

a church edifice without first getting a clear title to the
land. Any money collected under such conditions had
been falsely solicited.

Another point made clear to the field was that necessary
steps had already been taken to guarantee a sound title to
the land, if only the Trustees would go on with the building construction. It was made plain that Mr. Knapp was
fully ready to perform his part in giving a sound title, but
only on the terms of the deed itself, and only in accordance
with Mrs. Eddy's expressed wish as the donor. It was
made known to the field that Mrs. Eddy had begged the
Trustees to go on with the building construction, or else
to stop calling for funds under false pretenses.

The Trustees took the position, however, that they
would accept no title at all except on their terms, as outlined by their lawyer. To this Mrs. Eddy objected; and
on June 7, she made the request that the contributors be
advised to require the Trustees to start building, or to
return their money until such time as the title to the land
should be made sound. In this same letter, she advised
Mr. Knapp to let the Trustees get out of their difficulties
as best they could, and let *them* break the deed, inasmuch
as the deed contained the conditions of the gift of land.
She instructed him to refuse to do anything until they had
broken the deed.

On June 11, Mrs. Eddy wrote Mr. Knapp as follows:

"God will keep you, and when you hear His voice and can distinguish between the highest false sense that means well, and the 'still small voice' of Good, you will follow. Till then, God will lend me to you to distinguish for you what is the false and what the true direction. . . . The Trustees have fairly proven their unfitness for God's service, trustworthiness, which is the highest point of faith. . . . I *do hear* the voice of God, He does show me the way at all times. Oh! if the Trustees had only followed my directions at first, the house would now be going up and His cause honored and the title *made sound*."

Again on June 15, Mrs. Eddy wrote to Mr. Knapp, "Just as the Scriptures in Genesis and Revelation portray the *two sides*, so all revelation comes to me. I told you last evening the side that contest could carry on to a victory through a material hard fought battle. Today I tell you the other side so clearly revealed, namely, 'Be still and know that I am God' — I chose to take this side, and so do you. Now remain in watching and prayer, but take no legal steps toward breaking the deed, and sign no papers and give no pledges, orally or written, and let the Trustees meet the fearful sins that they alone commit."

Mrs. Eddy encouraged and reassured Mr. Knapp by writing to him on July 31, 1892: "You are experiencing the blows that have fallen on all true followers of Christ, and Jesus said 'Ye shall indeed drink of my cup'." Again she wrote on August 13, 1892, in reply to a letter from Mr. Knapp, "You are right. Theology, Materia Medica, Human law and lawyers are the scourges that lash the person of Jesus and would annul the Gospel. But we must meet them and be careful not to give them occasion to hate us more for Christ's sake. I thank God that through it all I have known that you could not be made to do wrong knowingly, or to flinch one single duty. You have suffered more than the others, only because you have been nearer the Master's life who drank this cup."

Up to this point, Mrs. Eddy had been urging the building of the church edifice as the one paramount issue; but everything seemed to obstruct the carrying out of that divine decree. And something hitherto hidden had to be uncovered to her. Now, for the first time, Mrs. Eddy had her attention called to the circular letter issued by the Trustees calling for contributions. In that letter, she saw for the first time, that the call was made for money to build a church which would include publishing rooms in the same edifice. This circular had been issued without Mrs. Eddy's knowledge or consent. The inclusion of publishing rooms in the church building was contrary to the provision in the deed, as we have already noted.

Thereupon, Mrs. Eddy requested Mr. Knapp and the Trustees to meet her in conference at Pleasant View, Concord, New Hampshire, on July 16, 1892. At that meeting

Mrs. Eddy asked her lawyers, in the presence of the Trustees and Mr. Knapp, "If advertising for funds to build publishing rooms gave any title to the church property?" (*The Christian Science Journal*, Vol. X, p. 274). Mr. Nixon promptly declared it did not. The lawyer replied emphatically that it did. From that moment, Mrs. Eddy said no more about using the funds on hand for building a church edifice. Although she had previously recommended that the contributors call on the Treasurer for the return of their donations, now she was convinced that the money must be returned to the contributors, and that the land must revert to Mr. Knapp. Once more must Mary Baker Eddy take up the perilous problem of lifting the thought of her students to the spiritual altitude essential to the building of a church edifice according to divine direction.

Mr. Lang, the Treasurer, had not taken out a bond as the deed required; and it was held that the conditions of the deed had been broken on that point. Thereupon, a deed to terminate the trust estate was signed early in August by the Directors and the Trustees; and on August 19, Mr. and Mrs. Knapp gave a quitclaim deed of the land to Mrs. Eddy. Although Mrs. Eddy had controlled the title to the land from the time she rescued the mortgage in 1889, it was not until this date, August 19, 1892, that she held the actual title in her own name.

VI

THE COMPLETION OF "OUR PRAYER IN STONE"

CHAPTER VI

---
*

The Completion of "Our Prayer in Stone"*

THE erection of the church edifice in Boston was still the dominant purpose in Mrs. Eddy's thought. A second time she had brought about a peaceful settlement of the difficulties of her Church; and for the third time, she was ready to go on with full faith that under divine direction her Church would be established. She prayed for divine Love to guide her in the discovery of human provisions for holding church property without returning to the old form of organization. Her Boston lawyers could find in their state laws no statute of the kind she needed. Then she engaged two lawyers in New Hampshire to search for such a Massachusetts statute.

Meanwhile, on August 22, 1892, invitations were issued to twelve Christian Scientists, selected by Mrs. Eddy, to meet and incorporate a Church, according to an agreement to which they had subscribed on August 17, 1892. Mrs. Knapp was one of the twelve students selected, and her invitation reads as follows:

---

* "Miscellaneous Writings," by Mary Baker Eddy (p. 141).

"*To* Flavia S. Knapp

"You are hereby notified that the first meeting of the subscribers to an agreement to associate themselves with the
intention to constitute a corporation to be known by
the name of First Church of Christ, Scientist, dated August 17th, 1892, for the purpose of organizing said Corporation, by adoption of the by-laws and election of officers
and the transaction of such other business as may properly
come before the meeting, will be held on Monday the
29th day of August, 1892, at 12 o'clock M., at No. 133
Dartmouth Street, Boston, Mass.

WILLIAM B. JOHNSON
one of the subscribers to said agreement.

Boston, Mass., *August* 22, 1892."

Had Mrs. Eddy at last permitted her Church to reorganize? If so, it would be in agreement with her letter to
Mr. Knapp of May 11, 1892: "Let the Church reorganize
if she thinks best . . . let her pass on to her experience, and
the sooner the better. When we will not learn in any
other way, this is God's order of teaching us. His *rod
alone* will do it." Mrs. Eddy was at last willing to go with
the church members in this perilous experiment, if only
it would be a means of getting the church building actually
started.

Meanwhile, however, the New Hampshire lawyers, who

proved to be amenable to spiritual guidance, had discovered a Massachusetts statute providing for donees, who could hold property in trust for a church, without requiring a church to incorporate. God had rewarded Mrs. Eddy's devotion to His Cause! On the authority of this newly found statute, she had a second trust deed drawn up, the one which now appears in the Manual of The Mother Church. When she wrote her first trust deed, she evidently had some misgivings as to the outcome, inasmuch as she provided that the title to the church lot should revert to Mr. Knapp in case of any breach of the trust. Now her method was masterly, unfaltering, with no such provision for retracing footsteps.

The meeting took place, according to the notice, in Miss Julia Bartlett's rooms on Dartmouth Street. Mrs. Eddy, however, sent Dr. Foster Eddy to the meeting to tell those present that she had decided not to organize a corporation. Instead, she instructed him to present to the meeting the new trust deed, which had been drafted by the New Hampshire lawyers but not yet executed, and which conveyed the lot for the church building to four donees. The deed provided that these donees, three of whom had belonged to the previous Board of Directors, namely, Ira O. Knapp, William B. Johnson, and Joseph S. Eastaman, should constitute a body corporate. Stephen A. Chase of Fall River, Massachusetts, was named as the fourth donee.

The deed was read at this meeting, the four grantees being among those present. Thereupon, in obedience to Mrs. Eddy's request, it was voted without dissent to accept the four grantees of the deed as Directors of her Church. When Mrs. Eddy was informed of the action taken at the meeting, she had the deed executed on September 1, 1892.

The next meeting of the twelve members was called by Mr. Johnson for September 23, at Mrs. Eddy's request in a letter which also contained instructions to elect a chairman and secretary. "Then," she added, "vote yourselves, chairman included, members of The First Church of Christ, Scientist." Further instructions from Mrs. Eddy requested them to vote themselves First Members of The First Church of Christ, Scientist. The meeting was duly held on September 23, 1892, at which those twelve students voted themselves, as Mrs. Eddy had requested, "First Members of The First Church of Christ, Scientist, in Boston, Massachusetts." Their names were as follows: Ebenezer J. Foster Eddy, Stephen Asa Chase, Joseph S. Eastaman, William B. Johnson, Ira O. Knapp, Julia S. Bartlett, Mary W. Munroe, Ellen L. Clark, Mary F. Eastaman, Janet T. Colman, Flavia S. Knapp, Eldora O. Gragg. Officers were chosen at this meeting, and certain tenets and rules for the government of the Church were adopted. Thus was started on a scientific and permanent foundation, and without an incorporated organization, The First Church of Christ, Scientist. This Church, with its unique form of government, has from that date continued its successful challenge to sin and sickness.

Mrs. Eddy had now given to her Church a sound title and a form of government, but there were no funds for building. The fund held by the former Trustees had been returned to the contributors, except a small amount which was uncalled for, and which Mr. Lang finally turned over to Stephen A. Chase, the new Treasurer of the Board of Directors.

The new Directors issued their first call for funds in a circular letter, dated September 16, 1892; and on January 13, 1893, Mr. Chase stated that $30,416.26, an amount about equal to that collected by the former Trustees, had already been contributed to the new building fund. This response from the field to aid in building an edifice to be used exclusively for a church, justified Mrs. Eddy's comment that she was "confident that all loyal Christian Scientists will gladly consecrate our Church to a more dignified end than an exchange, or a place for business bickerings, bag and baggage!" (*The Christian Science Journal*, Vol. X, p. 274). In reply, the students sent Mrs. Eddy a vote of thanks for having once more rescued them from a grave situation, and for having placed the building fund on a sound basis.

Mrs. Eddy then sent letters to forty-two of her students,

counting husband and wife as one, requesting them to subscribe one thousand dollars each to the building fund. The significance of this request does not appear on the surface; for most of that number were in rather limited financial circumstances. Perhaps not more than a dozen of them could at the moment have drawn a check for a thousand dollars. It meant, therefore, that Mrs. Eddy had by invitation enlisted this group of Christian Scientists to do the most efficient metaphysical work of which they were capable, in order to raise their quota for the building fund. The result was that these metaphysicians, under Mrs. Eddy's leadership, succeeded in establishing for all time the proof that the spontaneity of unlimited supply is the normal fact.

Mr. Joseph Armstrong of Piqua, Ohio, a student of Mrs. Eddy's who had been a banker, and who possessed sound business experience, succeeded Mr. Nixon on January 1, 1893, as Manager of The Christian Science Publishing Society. Not long after Mr. Armstrong's arrival in Boston, Mr. Eastaman resigned as Director, and Mr. Armstrong was appointed in his place. As Mr. Lang had been selected under the former plan to direct the construction of the church edifice, so now Mr. Armstrong was given charge of the building operations.

In November, 1893, the work of laying the church foundation was actually begun. It seemed as if Christian

Science, by its challenge to sin, had arrayed the forces of evil against the progress of the building. However, the Directors broke through one obstruction after another, until on May 21, 1894, the corner-stone of the edifice was actually laid.

In a letter to Mr. Knapp of May 28, 1894, Mrs. Eddy said: "If you keep in your own hands the work God has entrusted to you, all will be well. For you will, can, hear His voice and follow, and none can pluck you out of His hands." Mr. Knapp's reply to Mrs. Eddy included a description of the laying of the corner-stone, and is as follows:

"279 Columbus Ave.,
Boston, Mass.
May 29, 1894

"*My beloved Teacher:*

"Your inspiring letter is just at hand. It is the declaration of Spirit and Truth: and I do pray that we may be led and fed and sustained unto the end and completion of this great work which God has given us to do; for without the guidance and protection of God through divine wisdom and understanding, we cannot raise the human, material symbol of Church or manhood above the false claims of sin and error which seem to beset us on every hand. But these false claims have no authority from God, therefore they must all give place to the divine Idea of Christian

Science, which establishes the claims of Truth and Love on earth as in heaven. The Corner Stone of this spiritual building is laid upon the iron bands which circle humanity with the strength of divine Principle as revealed in Christian Science. Thus may it stand through a time and times of revelation, and the half of a time which seems to hang betwixt heaven and earth in the last day; then is the work finished on earth as all is in the heaven of eternal Principle — Life and Love forever.

"Let me relate the picture of that day we laid the Corner Stone. I was there in the morning. The workmen said the stone could not be laid for five days. I showed the foreman how it could be done that day, and promised a reward if he would carry out the plan. He changed his voice and said it could be done, and that he would work to that end if it took until late in the day. I was there nearly all the time, directing even where it did not seem my place to do so. But the stone was laid, which contains all your works on Christian Science; and a little before the seventh hour, in the twilight of the evening, the three Directors consecrated the event as you had directed us to do. So with one hand upon the Stone, our heads uncovered and faces toward the western sky, where the clouds of the weary day were disappearing, we stood in silent communion with God, followed with the Lord's Prayer in unison, as we lifted our voices upon the stillness around us.

Thus may it rest until God's purpose is finished on earth as it is in heaven.

Lovingly yours,

IRA O. KNAPP."

There were only three Directors present at the laying of the corner-stone, because Mr. Johnson was in Pittsburgh, trying to break through the blockade which was holding up the delivery of the steel so essential to the construction of the church.

Mr. Armstrong's book, "The Mother Church," which describes so admirably the building of the original edifice, tells of the mighty struggles which the Directors endured in carrying their Herculean task to completion. It tells of the intrepid Leader, arousing, encouraging, admonishing the Directors, when again and again it seemed impossible to continue the building. Earnest students of Christian Science should not fail to read Mr. Armstrong's book. They can recognize in this book that the author was a metaphysician who had seen his Leader's place in Bible prophecy, as his obedience to her every command so clearly indicated. The building of the church had to be done in the face of the very evil which the challenge of the Church had already aroused. But God was aiding this enterprise for the establishment of His kingdom on earth, and each time, through spiritual inspiration and strength the blockade was broken, and the work went forward.

It would be impossible for any other church building to meet with the opposition which the erection of The Mother Church encountered, for no other church edifice can ever symbolize in the same distinctive sense the spiritual idea of Church.

The evil influence, which the Directors encountered in building The Mother Church, has long been called animal magnetism. Mrs. Eddy has characterized it in "Miscellaneous Writings" as "a bland denial of Truth" (p. 31). That animal magnetism is not a modern invention is proved by St. Paul's reference to it, when he declares: "The good that I would I do not: but the evil which I would not, that I do." Indeed, the book of Job, which is supposed to be the oldest book in the Bible, records the operations of animal magnetism and how to overcome it. All this indicates that the "bland denial of Truth" has been asserting itself ever since the divine sense of good began to expose the nature of evil. This obstructive, animal influence is nothing to be feared, however, but like all sin, it must be recognized in order to be destroyed.

Paul proved his ability to distinguish between his own thought of God's goodness on the one hand, and the "bland denial" of it on the other, when he declared: "The law of the Spirit of life in Christ Jesus hath made me free from the law of sin and death." Other Christian worthies, however, such as Martin Luther, have unquestionably grasped the Christ, Truth; but when the "bland denial" of that truth began to assert itself in their thought, they often accepted the denial, and so lost the truth they had gained. Mrs. Eddy's early students who had seen and acknowledged the truth of Christian Science, especially those who held church office, were buffeted in the same way, until some of them grew indifferent to the truth, and finally deserted the Cause.

This failure of her students to hold to the truth was most disheartening to Mrs. Eddy, until she gathered around her the four Directors who stood faithful during the building of The Mother Church. These Directors, together with Judge Septimus J. Hanna, who was during that period editor of *The Christian Science Journal*, were her first students who could successfully hold church office in the face of that "bland denial" of what they knew to be true in the sight of God. They were destined to remain faithful to the end of their earthly lives; and of the twelve First Members who reorganized the Church, Dr. Foster Eddy was the only one who left it.

Mrs. Eddy once wrote to Mr. Knapp: "Oh, do not sleep again, do not let the word go forth 'sleep on and take thy rest,' 'mine hour hath come.' You will always think you are fully *aroused* to the present need when the glamor is deepest. You are always most safe when you realize you are in need of more conscious truth relative to the lie, and *its action*, and feel sure it is nothing, and His strength abounding in you, and see the path of the serpent and handle the error without fear. . . .

"The birth out of matter into spirit is not gained by *argument*, nor by force. It is *growth, hourly;* it is forever getting nearer Love that *is Love:* universal, divine *presence* and power, alias *might* and dominion; first over the body; then its reflection is dominion over all the earth."

It is well to remember that all Mrs. Eddy has written about the temporary nature of organization was said of that church organization which she abandoned in 1889. Through her inspired leadership, she proved that church property can be held without being encumbered by a material organization; and on the spiritual foundation which she established, The Mother Church edifice was finally erected. Services were held in the new church on the last Sunday of that memorable year, 1894, and the church was dedicated on January 6, 1895.

Mrs. Eddy made her first visit to the church on April 1, 1895, going directly to Mother's Room, which occupied the tower on the auditorium floor, and in which she remained overnight. Her next visit to The Mother Church was on Sunday, May 26, 1895, and this time she occupied the pulpit and addressed the congregation. She entered the auditorium during the reading of the Lesson-Sermon. The audience arose to welcome her, and she spoke to them with great earnestness for about twenty minutes. She then returned to her room in the tower. At the conclusion of the service, she met by invitation some of her students in the vestibule adjoining her room, and exchanged greetings with them. In the afternoon she returned to her home in Concord, New Hampshire.

Of the great events that transpired in the year 1895, the dedication of The Mother Church edifice ranks foremost. At that time Mrs. Eddy abolished personal preaching, and ordained the Bible and "Science and Health with Key to the Scriptures" as the Pastor over The Mother Church. The new order of services provided for two Readers instead of a preacher. The first appointees were Judge Septimus J. Hanna, First Reader, and Mrs. Eldora O. Gragg, Second Reader, who served for over seven years. Then the three-year term for Readers in The Mother Church was established by Mrs. Eddy.

In that same eventful year of 1895, there appeared for the first time the "Manual of The Mother Church," of which Mrs. Eddy has said in "The First Church of Christ, Scientist, and Miscellany": "Notwithstanding the sacrilegious moth of time, eternity awaits our Church Manual, which will maintain its rank as in the past, amid ministries aggressive and active, and will stand when those have passed to rest" (p. 230).

VII

FURTHER DEVELOPMENTS IN THE
SPIRITUAL REALM

CHAPTER VII

---✷---

Further Developments in the Spiritual Realm

IT was Mrs. Eddy's belief that, if she could make an arresting point with a stranger at the first interview on Christian Science, she could usually hold that one's interest in this Science. The experience of one of her students, Mrs. Janette E. Weller, is a case in point. Mrs. Weller was having her first interview at Mrs. Eddy's home on Columbus Avenue, when Mrs. Eddy said rather abruptly, "If mortal mind agreed that a man's gray matter were in his great toe, then he would do his thinking in his great toe." This is rather startling for a beginner to hear; but Mrs. Eddy continued with another radical statement, "But for the claim of animal magnetism, I could walk right out of this window without falling."

An explanation of such technique is given in the Christian Science textbook as follows: "If it becomes necessary to startle mortal mind to break its dream of suffering, . . . afterwards make known to the patient your motive for this shock, showing him that it was to facilitate recovery" (Science and Health, p. 420). The effect of that technique on Mrs. Weller was to awaken in her a loyalty and friend-ship for her Leader which were never broken.

We gain another side light on Mrs. Eddy's technique from her adopted son, Dr. Foster Eddy. He had a sunny disposition, enjoyed people, and was very companionable. He made it known that he had a great desire to be the First Reader of The Mother Church. Mrs. Eddy's reason for not satisfying his wish is very revealing. After per-mitting him to substitute for the regular Reader for three weeks (October 1 to 28, 1895), she discovered that, humanly speaking, he had a mesmerizable mind, and that the enemy might try to use his knowledge of medicine to harm the congregation. So she resolutely refused to sanction his appointment as Reader of her Church.

However, the enemy set another trap for him when he was the publisher of Mrs. Eddy's writings. As soon as the difficulty was recognized, it was thought desirable for him to get away from the limelight as much as possible, and it was arranged for him to stay at the home of Mr. and Mrs. Knapp. In a letter to Mr. Knapp, asking for a monthly bill of her son's expenses, Mrs. Eddy added: "I hope the atmosphere at your house, and this retreating from the fire at the fort of God, will be blessed to him." Again, she wrote to Mrs. Knapp, "Words can never express duly the gratitude I owe you for your perpetual kindness to me and my son. Nothing but the spirit of Christ could cause you to work and watch as you have done. You seem like the family in Bethany where our blessed Master found rest and sympathy." Referring to their united strength, she wrote to Mr. Knapp, "I speak of the you and Mrs. Knapp whom God hath joined together."

After spending a year in the Knapp household, Mrs. Eddy sent her son to live with Judge and Mrs. Hanna, at the First Reader's residence, 385 Commonwealth Avenue, Boston. A year with them failed to heal the difficulty, because Foster Eddy was both vain and lazy. He was then sent to Philadelphia, where he was expected to devote himself to the work of a practitioner. Gradually he drifted away from Christian Science entirely, and returned to his former home in Vermont, where he rejoined the Methodist church.

Meanwhile, some of Mrs. Knapp's relatives began to manifest an interest in Christian Science, and the first one to turn wholeheartedly to this Science was her eldest brother. He was confined to his bed with a belief of rupture and, in order to save his life, the physicians said that he must have an operation. Instead, he turned to his sister for help.

While he was being treated, Mrs. Knapp wrote to Mrs. Eddy about his case, and received the following reply: "The case named of rupture is considered very difficult, but God says all things are possible to Him. You have only to rouse yourself from a stagnant sense of God's power and presence. . . . Never yield for a moment to doubt or dismay. . . . God is perhaps trying you as He has tried all His own, and if you stand the test, all at once you will come into the kingdom of our Lord, a clear and abiding sense of your power to heal. Only be faithful over a few things and He will make you ruler over many, and then you will enter into the joy of your work. Rupture is only a thought of matter, but there is *no matter* and man's entire substance is Spirit. *Rouse* yourself from the dream of matter, and pluck the beam out of your own eye; help others and you are helping yourself; help yourself and you will help others. You know what I taught you is true. Now do not let the *enemy sow tares* while you *sleep* — be awake, and watch. Deny with all boldness that you cannot heal, for to admit it is dishonoring God, since He it is who heals, worketh through us, and we must see that we *reflect* Him, — reflect the divine power. I know, my dear students, the way is the way of our Master, full of crosses and crowns. I have more to meet than my students, so much more, you cannot conceive of my cup. But still I drink it, thankful that I am found worthy to suffer for Christ.

"Work right on, dear Mrs. Knapp, take pay for your labor, for the laborer in this cause is worthy of his hire, and God has employed you and He will *pay* you sure."

Evidently a great sense of responsibility was lifted when Mrs. Knapp learned she was not employed by the patient, but by God, and that He is always a sure paymaster. And because Love "beareth all things" (I Cor. 13:7), she dropped her personal responsibility, and telegraphed her brother to come to Boston. Although he was confined to his bed, he obeyed the summons, got out of bed, and took the night train for Boston. Within ten days after he reached Mrs. Knapp's home, his healing was complete; and his interest was so thoroughly established that he moved to Roslindale, and became a registered practitioner.

Mrs. Eddy's tasks as Leader of the Christian Science movement were increasing by leaps and bounds, and it became necessary for others to look after her material needs. Mrs. Knapp was one who frequently did her shopping for her. In a letter of gratitude to her for looking after such details, Mrs. Eddy said, "You are *growing*, advancing in truth and love. I feel it so plainly as I read your letters. Oh, may your life grow sweeter to your dear self as it does to Mother, and you be conscious of the growth, and perhaps you are. You cannot tell what a relief it is to me to read your letter. I have many dear ones who offer the same help, but who have not your ability."

Mrs. Knapp's ability was duly expressed in a home problem. Mr. Knapp discovered from the monthly report card of his son, Bliss, that he was not doing well in his school work.   Naturally, an explanation was required. When his father learned that the boy had been faithful in his studies, but that he was constantly saying the wrong thing when called upon to recite, even though he might know the right answer as soon as he was seated, Mr. Knapp saw through the difficulty immediately.   It was the old claim of animal magnetism which St. Paul describes in these words: "the good that I would I do not: but the evil which I would not, that I do."

Evidently Mr. Knapp was too busy at the moment to give his attention to the case, so he turned it over to his wife for healing in Christian Science.   The mother began to explain to her boy, with the greatest gentleness and consideration, why children go to school: it is not to learn a mass of facts, but rather to cultivate certain mental faculties.   She explained that some of the faculties of intelligence which he ought to cultivate were perception, reason, memory, application, and judgment.   Then, with the utmost patience, she told him how we grasp a new idea through the faculty of perception; how we take that idea into our understanding through the faculty of reason; how we retain it from being lost by the faculty of memory; and how we are able to express it to others through the faculties of application and judgment.

The next step was to make it clear that all these faculties

of intelligence belong to the divine Mind, for God is their creator; and as creations of the divine Mind, these faculties of intelligence are necessarily expressed in all of God's children alike. That gives to everyone an equal right to be a genius, and everyone can demand his divine right to express those faculties of intelligence. No human being ever claimed to be the author of memory; no human being ever claimed to be the originator of reason. God is their creator. Mrs. Eddy has explained in Science and Health (pp. 106 and 407), that God endowed man with reason as an inalienable right; and that "immortal memory" is never lost. This faculty psychology may not be in agreement with the schools, but it is in agreement with divine Science.

This loving mother continued to lead her son to recognize the source of his true intelligence, not in the human brain, but in the infinity of divine Mind. She made it clear that God's child, made in His image and likeness, must of necessity be made in the image and likeness of divine Mind; must of necessity be made in the image and likeness of His intelligence, including all the faculties of that intelligence. Therefore, in reality, this boy could no more be separated from the conscious reflection and activity of that intelligence than God could be lost or destroyed.

This explanation was repeated with varied amplifications each morning before school for about two weeks.

Thus the boy was led step by step to the inevitable conclusion that his God-bestowed faculties of intelligence were
inseparably related to the divine Mind. When he realized
how he was inseparably linked to God by reflection, he was
completely healed. From that time, it was easy for him
to recite in class correctly.

This experience strengthened the boy's mental faculties,
and gave him his first insight into what constitutes a
Christian Science treatment. At that early age, as a
grammar school pupil, he learned that a Christian Science
treatment is a well-reasoned, logical explanation of what
is true about God, and of man's relation to Him. When
that well-reasoned explanation was carried to the point of
realization or understanding, it brought the healing Christ
to human consciousness. In later years, he was increas-
ingly grateful that his mother had led him through the
actual footsteps of a Christian Science treatment up to
their healing fruitage, for those sacred ideals which she
planted remained to bless others.

Although Mrs. Knapp knew how to impart these sacred
truths to others, she shrank from holding regular classes in
Christian Science until Mrs. Eddy asked her to do so. A
class had been formed at Auburn, Maine, which Dr.
Foster Eddy was scheduled to teach. When Mrs. Eddy
heard of it, she decided that he must not go, and she asked
Mrs. Knapp to teach that class. It was on December 5,

1892, that Mrs. Knapp went to Auburn to teach her first class.

In the spring of 1895, Mr. and Mrs. Knapp moved from Roslindale to their new home in the Back Bay district of Boston, just two blocks from The Mother Church. The office on Columbus Avenue was discontinued, and they had their offices in the new home. Mrs. Knapp also taught her classes in Christian Science in the home.

Sometimes Mrs. Knapp consulted Mrs. Eddy about individuals who had applied for class instruction, and in April, 1895, Mrs. Eddy responded to such an inquiry by saying, "You may take each one you name into a class, and be strong and clear on the strong points. Do the best you can for them, and God will do the rest." Again in July, 1896, Mrs. Eddy wrote the following: "Yes, take the class you name. . . . Be careful to separate the old from the new, and empty the vessel you fill. No greater mistake can be made than to disobey or to delay to obey a single message of mine. *God* does speak through me to this age. This I discern more clearly each year of my sojourn with you."

Thus we learn that Mrs. Eddy was, about this time, discerning with increasing clarity her mission as a ruler in Israel. She had thought that "laws of limitation for a Christian Scientist," to use her own language, "would never be needed" (Miscellany, p. 229). But when the

Church Manual of The Mother Church began to function, she was blessed by a "grateful joy," because "Truth is strong with destiny" (*ibid.*). Finally, she knew that "Notwithstanding the sacrilegious moth of time, eternity awaits our Church Manual," because these By-laws "were impelled by a power not one's own" (Miscellaneous Writings, p. 148). Thus our Church Manual is as divinely authorized as is Science and Health. Therefore the Christian Scientist will obey the By-laws in our Church Manual as intelligently as he obeys "the scientific statement of being" in Science and Health.

Many new problems were forcing their attention upon Mrs. Eddy concerning her infant Church. The public needed to be better informed about this new religion, and its critics needed to be answered. By the turn of the century, Mrs. Eddy had introduced three institutional activities into her Church government to meet the growing demand for them. One of the new institutions was the Christian Science Board of Lectureship, whose members must "include in each lecture a true and just reply to public topics condemning Christian Science, and to bear testimony to the facts pertaining to the life of the Pastor Emeritus" (Manual, p. 93).

However, the lecture work was too general to deal effectively with the pulpit and the press. Critics of Christian Science seized upon those two avenues for attacking this new religion, and the attacks were going unanswered. Mr. Alfred Farlow of Kansas City, Missouri, watched those frequent attacks with growing concern, and finally he set about answering them, and his answers were published. Some of these attacks and his answers he sent to Mrs. Eddy, and she praised him for his work so ably done. She said in substance that his loyal defense of her would always enshrine him in her memory.

In January, 1899, Mrs. Eddy called Mr. Farlow to Boston to become the first general manager of the Committees on Publication for the Christian Science denomination. He was required by our Church Manual "to correct in a Christian manner impositions on the public in regard to Christian Science, injustices done Mrs. Eddy or members of this Church by the daily press, by periodicals or circulated literature of any sort" (Manual, p. 97).

Thus Mr. Farlow, who had already excelled as a practitioner and teacher of Christian Science in the Middle West, was now taken from the Board of Lectureship of The Mother Church in order to develop an efficient corps of assistants throughout the world to defend the Cause from specific attacks by the pulpit and the press. To this pioneer worker in this new field of activity was due in large measure an improved attitude of thought towards Christian Science and its Leader among newspapermen, and the intelligent public in general.

Mr. Farlow laid down a general plan for his assistants to follow in making replies to attacks, and in keeping in touch with all published matter, both for and against Christian Science. Although modest and retiring in character, he showed initiative and decisiveness in his new field of labor. He was an indefatigable worker, a clear thinker, and he had unusual ability in answering his critics satisfactorily and without bitterness. His work as Committee on Publication led to a more friendly attitude and much healing in the ranks of the opposition. In addition to his other duties, he was made President of The Mother Church for the year 1904.

The third institutional activity which Mrs. Eddy introduced into her form of Church government at this time was a Board of Education which should be an auxiliary to the Massachusetts Metaphysical College, which she had closed in the year 1889. The purpose of this Board of Education was to qualify competent teachers of Christian Science, and to insure their freedom from charlatanism.

The one whom Mrs. Eddy chose to pioneer in this field of activity was Mr. Edward A. Kimball. A prosperous manufacturer, he was healed of severe invalidism through Christian Science in 1887. He then turned wholeheartedly to the practice of Christian Science, was instructed in three different classes by Mrs. Eddy, and was made an original member of the Christian Science Board of Lectureship.

He served as its chairman continuously throughout his connection with the Board, and helped to establish many of the precedents which have continued to govern that Board.

Perhaps Mr. Kimball's chief contribution to our Cause was his work as the teacher of the Board of Education for five years, beginning with its first class in the year 1899. In that first class, he had three associate teachers, but afterwards one teacher was deemed sufficient. Our Church history has been notably enriched by such pioneer workers as Mr. Kimball. He combined a penetrating intellect with great kindliness. He possessed an unusual power of analysis, and could support his point of view with irresistible logic. Thus he could satisfy the intellect and also appeal to one's moral nature. Amply endowed with a delicious sense of wit and humor, he was very approachable, yet he carried himself with dignity and distinction. He possessed an extensive vocabulary, and he had a forceful yet persuasive style of speaking.

As a metaphysician, Mr. Kimball did many mighty works of healing. One of his patients, Mr. W. F. Barrett of Chicago, he raised from the dead. The restoration to life was complete and Mr. Barrett subsequently became a Christian Science practitioner for many years.

When these defensive and educational methods had been introduced into our Church government, the Church could then consolidate its gains, and move forward to richer progress.

Healing is the purpose of our Church Manual as well as of Science and Health. Sickness and discords of every kind are lawless. The Apostle Paul has said, "the law was our schoolmaster to bring us unto Christ" (Gal. 3:24). In like manner, the healing Christ is in our Church By-laws because they correct lawless conditions; and when we place the same radical reliance upon them as we do upon the requirements of "the scientific statement of being," the Christ healing will result.

We can learn more of Mrs. Eddy's technique by studying her methods in healing a case of the last enemy. It was the case of her secretary, Mr. Calvin A. Frye, as told by an eyewitness, Miss Clara M. S. Shannon. Mrs. Eddy sent Miss Shannon to Mr. Frye's room with a message for him. She found him lying on his back on the floor, apparently lifeless. When his condition was reported to Mrs. Eddy, she went to his side, and talked aloud to him the truths of Christian Science. Her attitude at first was gentle and persuasive; she appealed to Mr. Frye by name in the most tender and loving manner; she declared he had work to do right here, and it was his duty to do it.

When Mr. Frye began to show signs of responding to her persuasion, Mrs. Eddy changed her mode of treatment quite abruptly. She was more masterful, and she made

demands upon him to defeat his enemies, because the Bible
teaches that death is indeed an enemy. This treatment
was given aloud, just as though he were in the full possession of his faculties and could understand what she was
saying.

Mrs. Eddy told Mr. Frye to rise to his feet, and she gave
him her hand to help him get up. Then she went out of
the room, and down a passage where she had been sitting.
She called to him, "Calvin, come here!" When he obeyed,
she spoke several minutes to him, striving to wake him up,
at times thundering against the error. Then she said,
"Now, you can go back to your room." When he had
gone a little way, she called him back, and talked the truth
to him again. This was repeated several times, until Miss
Shannon pleaded with her to let him sit down and rest.
Mrs. Eddy promptly denied the request. Then she told
him a story which made him laugh. When he laughed,
she said, "Thank God!" and then she let him go back to
his work.

Mrs. Eddy then explained some of her technique to quiet
Miss Shannon's troubled thought. When one is being
brought back from the symptoms of death, he may appear
to be dazed like one who is frozen, and it is not safe to
leave him in such a condition until an emotional experience can break the tension. Some simple expedient
should be attempted to make him laugh, cry, or get angry.

Mrs. Eddy's first effort was to make Mr. Frye angry; but when that failed, she got him to laugh; the tension was broken, and the work of resurrection was completed.

It is indeed heartening to know that Mrs. Eddy could raise the dead. The Bible records indicate that Elijah, Elisha, Daniel, Jesus, Peter, and Paul all overcame death through their understanding of the Fatherhood of God. Now that the Motherhood of God has been revealed to us through Christian Science, experience has proved that women as well as men can defeat the last enemy and raise the dead.

VIII

THE "EXCELSIOR EXTENSION" OF
THE MOTHER CHURCH

CHAPTER VIII

✱

The "Excelsior Extension" of The Mother Church

WE MAY recall that the Board of Directors of The Mother Church served as trustees for the church property, but that the other business of the Church was administered by the First Members in accordance with the provisions of the Church Manual. But certain potential dangers began to appear from having the church affairs administered by so large a group as the First Members had become. Various cliques sprang into being, each dominated more or less by some strong-minded leader, and these few leaders were apparently running the Church. After one important meeting, Mrs. Eddy required each First Member to write her a letter giving the exact reason for voting as he did at that meeting. Some frankly admitted that their votes were influenced by some member whose judgment they respected. These answers, together with other considerations, caused Mrs. Eddy to change the By-laws so as to remove all business from the control of the First Members, and place it in the hands of the Board of Directors.

One of these strong-minded First Members was Mrs. Augusta E. Stetson of New York City. Well knowing that the Directors must be alert to such a subtle influence, Mrs. Eddy sounded a note of warning in a letter to Mr. Knapp which read in part as follows: "Mrs. Stetson has a church of her own to care for, and must not and shall not control my church and treat my students in it as she does and has in New York. . . . But I can bear, 'and open not my mouth,' much — and yet I shall hope this disloyalty will stop soon, for God will not suffer it beyond a 'hither and no farther'. " In a later communication she said, "You will sometime learn Mrs. Stetson's motives." One of her motives was to succeed Mrs. Eddy as the Leader of the Christian Science movement, and she let it be known that so long as Mrs. Eddy continued to live, she was depriving Mrs. Stetson of her destiny.

In March, 1898, Mrs. Knapp passed on quite suddenly, and Mrs. Stetson tried to get control of her most promising students. As a warning to one such student, Rev. Irving C. Tomlinson, Mrs. Eddy said, "Doing as I would be done by, I write you, seeing as I do the attempt of error on all who have lost their class instructor.

"You named a word that opened your thought wherein I read what you do not know, even the means used to ensnare or get you into her ranks, and use you as a despot only so long as you subserve her personal purpose to rule, then cast you off and herself string the fish you have caught. Beware! never come under *her influence*. She is as far from your former teacher as the sky from dust."

Mrs. Eddy said further to Mr. Tomlinson, "Your dear teacher, Mrs. Knapp, was one of my best students, and had she remained with us, it was my intention to make her the teacher of the Massachusetts Metaphysical College."

While Mrs. Eddy was safeguarding others, she was at the same time doing all in her power to heal Mrs. Stetson. Knowing that nothing but the highest expression of love and compassion could save her, Mrs. Eddy probably poured out more love on that student than on any one else. Mrs. Stetson was given every consideration. The wheat and the tares were allowed to grow side by side until the harvest. This continued for thirteen years after the first warning to Mr. Knapp. Then Mrs. Stetson's pupils sent a letter to Mrs. Eddy in July, 1909, deifying their teacher's personality, and giving the letter their unqualified approval. That was enough to convince Mrs. Eddy that there was little hope of a healing (Miscellany, p. 359), and she requested the Directors to act upon the case.

One phase of Mrs. Stetson's error was to speak in the absolute, and answer people's questions by statements of absolute Science which she could not possibly demonstrate. This reminds us how Mrs. Eddy once rebuked another student by saying, "Come down. Your head is way up there in the stars, while the enemy is filling your body with bullets." It was rather difficult to know whether Mrs. Stetson was honest in what she said, but her students were intrigued by her pretensions, and placed her on a pedestal. During her trial, the newspapers treated her absolutism in a jocular manner, and described it by the story of "Johnnie and the Jam." Johnnie's weakness for jam caused him to visit the pantry frequently, until his mother told him to keep out of the pantry. One day she caught Johnnie in the very act of eating jam, and the evidence of it was smeared over his face. When she accused him of disobeying her orders, Johnnie, speaking in the absolute, denied that he had been eating jam. But when mamma spanked Johnnie, he did not cry in the absolute.

Christian Science teaches that there must be some acknowledgment of sin before it can be healed. Mrs. Stetson at her trial made no such acknowledgment, but denied every allegation against her. She brought a lawyer, who was one of her students, to safeguard her rights; and although he greatly admired her, the evidence presented at that trial caused him to repudiate his teacher, when his eyes had been opened to her crafty methods. Needless to say, Mrs. Stetson was dismissed from the Church.

Administering church discipline was an important part of the work which the Board of Directors inherited from the First Members. An early case of church discipline was that of a First Member who was charged with immoral conduct. From the evidence submitted, the Directors were convinced that the charges were sustained. They removed his practitioner's card from *The Christian Science Journal*, disqualified him as a First Member, and removed him from church membership. Instead of healing the individual, it made him so rebellious that he threatened a lawsuit in revenge.

When this case was brought to Mrs. Eddy's attention, she requested the Directors to restore all the privileges they had taken from him. The result was a complete healing of the individual, and a great lesson to the Directors who learned that the purpose of Christian Science is to save and not to destroy. As Jesus said, he came not "to destroy men's lives, but to save them" (Luke 9:56). When the next case of a similar nature was tried by the Directors, the erring member was lovingly admonished and placed on probation. By keeping him within the fold, he was rescued from his downward course.

Said Mr. Knapp on the topic of church discipline, "The understanding and practice of Christian Science is the greatest discipline for all mankind, and will be, so long as erring mortals seem to need correction. . . . Every Christian church has the moral and legal right to discipline its weak, indiscreet, or wicked members, but for the sole purpose of reforming them. . . . For one to commit the case of an offending church member to the cruel and uncivil court of gossip and public opinion, is a moral offense in itself."

Through these varied experiences, the Directors were growing more benevolent. Their breadth of vision was increasing, as the destiny of The Mother Church unfolded to them. Also their regard for each other increased with their years of experience together. They had their differences, to be sure, because they were men of strong convictions and decided traits of character. Nevertheless, each respected the other's honesty and sincerity, and there was a deep sense of affection among them. Stephen Chase, for example, was a diamond in the rough, but he showed his kindness to his fellow Directors in an interesting way. Each autumn it was his custom to buy the product of a choice grapevine in his vicinity, and to share the grapes with his brother Directors. He was quite a connoisseur of art, and acquired a number of oil paintings; above all, he was very tender-hearted, in spite of a brusque exterior; and his honesty was above reproach.

Early one morning, Mr. Chase came from his home in Fall River to see Mr. Knapp about some church business. It was the custom of the Knapp family to adjourn from the breakfast table to Mr. Knapp's office, where they read a portion of the Sunday Lesson, concluding with the Daily

Prayer from the Church Manual. Mr. Chase reached the house during this morning service, and he was invited to join the family group while the service continued. As he sat there, he was so deeply moved that he could not restrain his emotion, and the tears rolled down his cheeks. When the Daily Prayer was concluded, he hurried from the house without a word of explanation, and his business conference had to wait until the next day.

Mr. Chase had an abiding affection for Mrs. Eddy, and he would frequently burst into tears at the mention of her name, so deeply was his heart touched by her struggles and victories. He was a true follower of his Leader, because he had seen her place in Bible prophecy.

The membership of the Church and the local congregation had increased to such an extent that two Sunday services, and finally three, became necessary to accommodate those who attended the services. This influx of adherents forced the issue of building an extension of The Mother Church. The proposition was made in a practical way at the Annual Meeting of The Mother Church held in June, 1902, less than ten years after the present form of church government was instituted. Mr. Edward A. Kimball addressed the meeting by reading a motion calling for the erection of an extension of The Mother Church which would seat four or five thousand people, and pledging the members to contribute any amount up to two million dollars for this purpose. The motion was unanimously adopted.

Naturally, this pledge could not legally commit the Church to any definite action, but it did express the purpose of the members to provide a building commensurate with the dignity and growth of the Church. The four Directors who had built the original edifice, began at once to formulate plans for the new structure. Mr. Chase, the Treasurer, called for contributions to the building fund; and the remaining land in the triangular lot upon which The Mother Church stands, was purchased for the new building. The next thing was to secure the architect.

Mr. E. Noyes Whitcomb, a Christian Scientist whom Mrs. Eddy employed to build the Christian Science Church in Concord, New Hampshire, suggested an architect. This man had drawn the plans of a memorial church at Fairhaven, Massachusetts, which was regarded as an outstanding example of church architecture in its beauty of design and ornamentation. The Directors visited that church at Fairhaven, and were convinced that they had found just the right architect. This man, Mr. Charles Brigham, drew the plans which were finally accepted for The Mother Church extension.

In June, 1902, Judge Hanna resigned as editor of the Christian Science periodicals and as First Reader of The Mother Church, in order to serve on the Christian Science

Board of Lectureship. Mr. Archibald McLellan, of Chicago, succeeded him as editor. On February 7, 1903, Mr. McLellan was made a Director, which increased the membership of the Board to five. He also succeeded Mr. Knapp as chairman of the Board of Directors, and the old Board members, with their new chairman, went forward with the erection of the extension, the corner-stone of which was laid July 16, 1904.

Again the harassing problems of obstruction and delay had to be overcome; but this time the Directors had their past experiences to guide them. The construction company, which had the contract to build the auditorium floor, met with a threatened strike; whereupon this company secured an injunction from the court restraining the trade unions employed on the building from strikes, and including the Board of Directors in its restraining order, as a protection in their construction job. That injunction actually benefited the Directors immensely, because the auditorium floor was one of the last jobs to be completed, and they were not troubled with any other labor difficulties during the building of the extension.

However, something formidable was arising in another direction. The original plan called for the completion of the building in June, 1907. As the work proceeded, Mrs. Eddy probed the mental horizon, only to discover that her enemies were evolving a deep-seated plot which must be foiled. The opposition was organized in two ways: one was intended to smear Mrs. Eddy's character through the press; and the other was to institute legal proceedings, the ultimate purpose of which was to declare her mentally incompetent, and thereby get control of the copyrights to Science and Health. The intention was to launch these attacks at the time of the dedication of the church edifice, so as to counteract any advantages which might accrue to the Cause from that event.

Like a wise general, Mrs. Eddy prepared herself for the assault. Her first move was to ask the Directors to advance by one year the dedication of the church building, that is to say, to June, 1906. The Directors consulted the architect and builder, only to be informed that the requirement was humanly impossible. Other men eminent in the building profession were consulted, and all agreed that such a request could never be carried out. But the Directors were taking orders from God's messenger, and they knew only too well that whatever God required of them was not only possible, but it must be achieved.

The Directors then stopped canvassing human opinions, and addressed themselves to this case as they would have worked for a patient who had been given up by the doctors as incurable. They saw that mortal mind had to be convinced that all things are possible with God. Soon afterwards, the builder ventured his belief that the work could be done in the allotted time. The next one to give his consent to the possibility was the architect's chief assistant, who was directing the work. The architect himself was unyielding. He would not admit that such an undertaking could be accomplished in the specified time.

The Directors were no more baffled by that obstruction than they would have been in the healing of a sick man. In this case, however, the architect was already sick; and not being a Christian Scientist, his physicians ordered him to take a trip to the Bermuda Islands for his health. That left his chief assistant, who had agreed that the work could be done in the allotted time, in complete charge of the construction. From that time, the work went forward, and the world knows today that The Mother Church extension was dedicated, free from debt, in June, 1906, one year earlier than the original date.

About three months before the time set for dedication, the Directors selected two good Christian Science practitioners, James J. Rome and John H. Thompson, to serve as watchmen at the church. They served part of every night until the dedication. In a letter which Mr. Rome wrote to Mrs. Eddy, he said in part (Miscellany, p. 61): "At first I thought that, since it seemed impossible for the building to be completed before the end of summer, the communion would likely be postponed until that time. Then came the announcement that the services would be held in the new extension on June 10.   I saw at once that somebody had to wake up.   I fought hard with the evidence of mortal sense for a time; but after a while, in the night, as I was climbing over stones and planks and plaster, I raised my eyes, and the conviction that the work would be accomplished came to me so clearly, I said aloud, 'Why, there is no fear; this house will be ready for the service, June 10.'   I bowed my head before the might of divine Love, and never more did I have any doubt.

"One feature about the work interested me.   I noticed that as soon as the workmen began to admit that the work could be done, everything seemed to move as by magic; the human mind was giving its consent.   This taught me that I should be willing to let God work.   I have often stood under the great dome, in the dark stillness of the night, and thought, 'What cannot God do?' (Science and Health, p. 135.)

"As I discovered the many intricate problems which must necessarily present themselves in such an immense undertaking, I appreciated as never before the faithful, earnest work of our noble Board of Directors.   With unflinching faith and unfailing fidelity they have stood at the breastworks in the battle, and won the reward, 'Well done, good and faithful servant; . . . enter thou into the joy of thy Lord'."

The enemies of Christian Science could not hasten their

attack by more than six months. So the church dedication took place in June under the most favorable circumstances; and not until the following December could the enemy launch its press attack, and the lawsuit, known as "The Suit of the Next Friends." Mrs. Eddy's son and her adopted son joined as plaintiffs in this lawsuit. The Directors and several other Christian Scientists who were close to Mrs. Eddy were named with her as co-defendants.

That Mrs. Eddy was well aware of the situation is evident from a letter which she wrote to Mr. Knapp on November 21, 1906, as follows: "Write to Bliss to make no more engagements to lecture at present, but to return and remain in Massachusetts till our next annual meeting in June. There is a great need of such as he is in Christian Science to be in Boston." Upon his arrival in Boston, Mrs. Eddy wrote to him under date of November 28, 1906, in part as follows: "I am glad you are near us. You are needed here more than elsewhere. Boston and Concord are the garrisons which need to be armored and defended."

Turning to Science and Health, we find an allegory known as the "Liver Trial," which begins on page 430. Beginning at line 22 of that page, Mrs. Eddy designates the members of the jury. During the lawsuit against her, she named one of the jurors in Science and Health as "Next Friends." After the suit was withdrawn, she took out of Science and Health the name "Next Friends," and put in

its place the words, "Greed and Ingratitude." Thus did
Mrs. Eddy designate the nature of the Next Friends' lawsuit.

However, that trial convinced Mrs. Eddy that she would
be more secure under the Massachusetts courts than she
had been under those in New Hampshire. This was one
of the deciding factors which caused her soon afterwards
to remove from Concord, New Hampshire, to make her
home at Chestnut Hill, near Boston.

About that time another important and far-reaching
factor in her form of church government was causing Mrs.
Eddy much prayerful consideration. It concerned the
requirement of her signature for the execution of certain
important By-laws in her Church Manual. She knew
that God had dictated to her those By-laws, and was this
requirement of her signature God's way of perpetuating
the Manual, because of the inseparability of the message
and the messenger? But if for any valid reason her signature could no longer be obtained, would that fact
under human law invalidate those By-laws, and therefore
the Manual?

For information as to what the human law would
support under such circumstances, Mrs. Eddy consulted
her lawyer, Samuel J. Elder, who was well versed in the
law concerning copyrights and legal trusts. He assured
her that a legal trust, such as The Mother Church, would

not be nullified in the event that her signature could no longer be obtained. Human law does not require the impossible in such matters, and therefore the impossibility of obtaining her signature would not nullify the execution of the By-laws in question.

This judgment from Mr. Elder completely satisfied Mrs. Eddy as to the legality of requiring her signature for certain important By-laws. However, she admitted the mental weight she might have to carry because of that personal link between herself and her Church Manual. That she was justified in her decision as to her signature has since been proved by the fact that the Supreme Judicial Court of Massachusetts has upheld that point of law which Mr. Elder gave to Mrs. Eddy, and has established for all time the legality of The Mother Church Manual.

The history of the Christian Science Church abundantly proves that persecutions have invariably strengthened the unity of the Scientists, and have increased their understanding of their Leader's place in Bible prophecy. The Directors also came in for their share of this devotion to the Cause. On the other hand, their duty in handling cases of discipline resulted in some animosity being heaped upon them. The situation was aptly described at the last interview which Mrs. Eddy held with her Directors at Chestnut Hill, when she said, "My Board of Directors are the most beloved and the most hated of all my students."

But she had already provided the remedy in these words from Science and Health: "Human hate has no legitimate mandate and no kingdom. Love is enthroned" (p. 454).

Mr. Knapp continued his arduous duties as a Director of The Mother Church, and as a member of the Bible Lesson Committee, until the time of his passing from this earthly experience on November 11, 1910, less than a month before the departure of his great Leader, whom he had served so faithfully and devotedly.

In a tribute written by his associate, Archibald McLellan, for the *Christian Science Sentinel* of November 19, 1910, we read: "Above all else, he was one who did those mighty works of healing which Jesus declared should be done by 'them that believe'." His fellow Directors also wrote for that same issue of the *Sentinel*, "His keen sense of justice, always tempered with mercy; his ready recognition of merit wherever it existed; and above all, his absolute and unfaltering devotion to our Leader, have been at all times a constant inspiration to those who have been associated with him.

"We rejoice in the knowledge that the qualities which Mr. Knapp manifested, and which have been impressed indelibly upon all who have known him, are eternal and cannot be lost, but must remain the real substance of his life work."

IX

AN APPRECIATION

By Judge Septimus J. Hanna

Mr. Bliss Knapp
My dear Friend:

I am inclosing the sketch of your father's life which I promised you. I realize that it is very inadequate, but the best I can do under the circumstances. It had to be more or less in the nature of my estimate of his character and relation to the work, as most of the facts within my knowledge were such that they cannot be mentioned.

Your father's greatest trials, severest tests, and mightiest triumphs were behind the scenes and can never be brought to light. I think you are sufficiently familiar with this to know what I mean. Nevertheless that part of his work known to the adherents of our movement, especially those who are pioneers, is enough to perpetuate his memory as one of Mrs. Eddy's most helpful supporters and disciples.

I did not feel that I could close this sketch without paying a brief tribute to your mother, because in their work they were so distinctly one, that we cannot talk or think of one without including the other.

Yours sincerely,

(*Signed*) S. J. HANNA

803 Oakland Ave.
Pasadena, Calif.
December 25, 1918

CHAPTER IX

*

An Appreciation

BY JUDGE SEPTIMUS J. HANNA

IT WAS my privilege to become acquainted with Mr. Ira O. Knapp in 1892, very soon after I became editor of *The Christian Science Journal*. Mr. Knapp was at that time a member of the Christian Science Board of Directors of The Mother Church, having been appointed to that position by the Reverend Mary Baker Eddy in September, 1892.

The Christian Science Board of Directors was constituted in the following way: Mrs. Eddy had long been hoping for a church edifice in Boston, and for several years her students had been making efforts to fulfill her hope. In 1887–1888 about four thousand dollars were contributed towards a building fund, but this money was lost. A site was bought; but as the students could give only a small part of the price, the remainder was secured by a mortgage. This they were unable to pay when it became due, and the lot was sold, under foreclosure, to Mrs. Eddy herself. She immediately conveyed it to Ira O. Knapp, C.S.D., for the use of the church, a Board of Trustees being appointed to care for it.

The sum of about thirty thousand dollars was soon raised, enough to warrant those trustees in beginning the work; but they were unwilling to build, unless the church, which had been disorganized at Mrs. Eddy's request, was reorganized, under the laws of Massachusetts; as, without such an incorporation, they claimed the title would be worthless.

Mrs. Eddy then took the lot again into her own possession, and deeded it, in September, 1892, to four of her students, thereby constituting them the Christian Science Board of Directors. This Board was to hold the land in trust for the whole body of Christian Scientists, a law having been discovered which permitted property to be held in this way. The new deed required the Directors to erect a church edifice within five years, at a cost of not less than fifty thousand dollars; and it was upon them, Ira O. Knapp, William B. Johnson, Joseph Armstrong, and Stephen A. Chase, and not upon the church as a body, that the responsibility of erecting the building rested ("History of The Mother Church," by Joseph Armstrong).

To be historically accurate, it is necessary to say that the deed of trust, making the conveyance above referred to, named Ira O. Knapp, William B. Johnson, Joseph S.

Eastaman, and Stephen A. Chase as Trustees. Mr. Eastaman having resigned his trusteeship, Mr. Armstrong was appointed to fill the vacancy, and in this way the Board of Directors of The Mother Church was constituted.

It will be seen from the above that Mr. Knapp had the confidence of Mrs. Eddy to such an extent that he was for a time made the sole trustee of the ground upon which the future church was to be erected, and that later he was named as one of the permanent Directors of The Mother Church.

When we consider the great responsibility devolving upon the Christian Science Board of Directors, we can easily see the confidence and trust Mrs. Eddy reposed in that body. They not only had charge of the building of The Mother Church edifice as it was originally constructed, and of the extension to it which was later built at an expense of upwards of two million dollars, but they were charged with the conduct of The Mother Church in all of its details, including the selection and appointment of all the subordinate officers necessary to such an organization. They were in no small degree also responsible for the organization and proper conduct of all branch churches which existed, and which were to be established in any part of the world. This responsibility extended also to the members of The Mother Church and, in a qualified degree, to all the members of the branch churches. In addition to these duties, cares, and responsibilities, there was much in the way of minor detail coming within the jurisdiction of this body that I will not here undertake to mention. It is not too much to say that as a whole the responsibilities and cares resting upon the shoulders of this Board were almost beyond human estimate or comprehension.

Mr. Knapp remained an active, faithful, and consecrated member of this official Board to the time of his death in 1910. Thus it will be seen that he served the Cause in that capacity for a period of eighteen years, during which time the Christian Science movement grew from a mere handful of adherents up into the millions, and the branch churches increased from a very few to thousands, so that the duties, cares, and responsibilities of the position expanded into almost inconceivable proportions.

Mr. Knapp's official activities, however, were not limited to his position as Director in The Mother Church. He was appointed to the responsible position of membership on the Bible Lesson Committee when this committee was first established, remaining as such to the time of his death.

Mrs. Hanna and myself were for a time members of that committee, and were thus associated with Mr. Knapp in this work, and hence I can speak from personal knowledge when I say that Mr. Knapp had much to do with building up the Bible Lessons, as published in the *Christian Science Quarterly*, to their present great proportions and efficacy. He, of course, had the benefit of the aid of his fellow-members, as well as the direct guidance for a number of years of our Leader, whose wisdom inaugurated and carried forward this wonderful method of preaching the gospel to all nations.

It is not amiss for me to say also that as editor of the periodicals and First Reader in The Mother Church, as well as in other capacities, I was brought into such intimate associations with Mr. Knapp, that of necessity I knew enough of his labor and consecration to our Cause to speak intelligently and appreciatively thereof.

Mr. Knapp was almost super-conscientious in the discharge of his duties, and this quality added to his sense of the weight of his responsibility. In addition to his official duties, Mr. Knapp carried a large number of patients, and thus put into practice his understanding of the teaching of Christian Science. This practical work and application of the Truth no doubt aided him greatly in bearing the burdens resting upon him in the discharge of his official duties.

Mr. Knapp's loyalty to our Leader and to all of her teaching, combined the simplicity of the little child with the strong adult character. I am aware that at times his loyalty was tested to the utmost limit, in ways which I cannot here mention, but he never for one moment wavered or yielded.

He was a consistent and persistent student of the Bible and of all of Mrs. Eddy's writings. His understanding of the Bible was deep and clear. He made a special study, I remember, of the Book of Revelation, and at times would give me interpretations of its spiritual meaning which were beyond my comprehension, until I took up the study of this book for myself, and then in some measure, at least, I was enabled to see as he saw. His knowledge, also, of our Leader's teaching was unusually profound. He arrived at his conclusions and conceptions only after the most painstaking study, never holding to hasty or superficial views, which often prove so mischievous. This made him a true Christian Scientist and a sage counselor. Although not learned in all the technical knowledge of the colleges and universities, he was nevertheless a deep student, and I regarded him as a well educated man. Indeed, super-adding his thorough knowledge of the Bible and our Leader's writings to his early education in the funda-mentals of human knowledge and his wide experience in practical affairs, I do not hesitate to pronounce him a scholar, and as such I think he should stand in history.

One could not look upon his face without seeing plainly depicted there the qualities of honesty, humanity, kindli-ness and compassion, faith, meekness and temperance, coupled with great firmness of conviction and fidelity. His spiritual nature was of a high order, and his domestic relations of the most exemplary kind.   In my association with him extending over a number of years, I never had occasion to question the sincerity of his motives in any respect or to adversely criticize any of his acts.   He may at times have been apparently over-tenacious of his own views, and thus, humanly speaking, the victim of strong self-will, but this was due rather to his deep conviction of the right, than to any vain-glorious egotism.

His tender regard for our Leader and her work was touching in its simplicity and depth.   In this respect he stood as a shining example.   He had no aim or purpose in life, after adopting Christian Science, than to aid in promoting it.   What he really achieved in this direction is known only to those familiar with his inner life, and they can only dimly apprehend it now.   The future will unfold it more and more as our Leader's great work for God and humanity becomes better understood, and the aid and support given to her by her pioneer students is more intelligently appreciated.   In view of my association and acquaintance with Mr. Knapp as above indicated, I can most heartily endorse what Mr. Archibald McLellan said of him in the *Christian Science Sentinel* of November 19, 1910, announcing his passing on: "In every one of his various relations to the church and to his fellow-men, Mr. Knapp's wholehearted service earned the 'Well done, good and faithful servant,' and he was greatly loved and esteemed by the entire field of Christian Scientists."

I recall some very interesting talks I had with Mr. Knapp. We were then living at 385 Commonwealth Avenue and Mr. Knapp's home was within easy walking distance. We would walk through the beautiful Back Bay Fens, usually on Sunday afternoons. Our talks, of course, related to Christian Science and Mrs. Eddy, and current matters in connection with the work. In one of these talks Mr. Knapp told me of a vision he had had after becoming Mrs. Eddy's student. At that time he was living on his farm in New Hampshire. This vision from any ordinary standpoint, was so unusual and significant, that I deem it worthy of a place in this sketch.

Mr. Knapp said in substance that he was in the habit of taking his Bible under his arm and seating himself under a large tree near his house. There he would study the Scriptures, and especially Revelation. One day while thus reading, when he was wide-awake and the sun shining full upon him, he saw in vision a large city and in the city a beautifully illuminated street. He had no conception of the meaning or significance of the vision, but in a casual way related it to Mrs. Eddy, when Mrs. Eddy was for a few days a guest in the home of the Knapps in New Hampshire. Mrs. Eddy seemed much pleased and interested in what he said, and remarked, "I understand," but offered no explanation.

After this event, the Knapps having exchanged their farm in New Hampshire for a residence in Roslindale near Boston, Mr. Knapp was on his way from one station in Boston to another station to take the train for Roslindale, and passing along Columbus Avenue, he saw the street that had appeared to him in this vision. The impression was so vivid and the resemblance so striking, that he at once connected the vision with the fact, and felt that it was on this street that he must establish himself in his spiritual work. Mrs. Eddy was at that time making her headquarters on Columbus Avenue, teaching her classes and conducting the movement from there. This no doubt sufficiently explains Mr. Knapp's vision, and the reason why he established his office near Mrs. Eddy's headquarters. Then after living for a while in Roslindale, the Knapps removed to Boston, making their home at Number 4 Batavia Street near The Mother Church.

This incident clearly shows that those who awaken in degree to their relation to God and His idea, are as distinctly directed and guided in modern times as the ancients were. Mrs. Eddy in her own experience proved this in many instances.

I do not feel that I should close this sketch without paying a brief tribute to the memory of Mrs. Flavia S. Knapp, the faithful spouse of Ira O. Knapp. She co-labored with Mr. Knapp intimately and effectively from the time they began their Christian Science work to the time of her passing on. She devoted her whole time and purpose to the spiritual work, teaching and healing. I know of no one who kept more closely to the fundamental teaching of Mrs. Eddy than did Mrs. Knapp. Her loyalty to Mrs. Eddy and her teaching was steadfast and intense. This, of course, enabled her to do successful healing work. I know whereof I affirm when I say that Mrs. Eddy had no students whom she trusted more implicitly than she did Mr. and Mrs. Knapp. Mrs. Hanna and myself always felt absolutely sure of them under the severely trying circumstances through which at times we jointly passed.

The history of the Christian Science movement would not be complete if due recognition were not given to the consecrated and self-sacrificing labors of these students of our Leader.

X

THE CHURCH TRIUMPHANT

CHAPTER X

---------------------------*---------------------------

*The Church Triumphant

WHEN SIMON PETER declared that Jesus was the Christ, the Master promptly forestalled any assumption that Peter's declaration might come from an emotional impulse by his immediate reply, "Flesh and blood hath not revealed it unto thee, but my Father which is in heaven." On that spiritual recognition of the Christ, Jesus proposed to build his Church. On page 583 of "Science and Health with Key to the Scriptures," Mary Baker Eddy defines "Christ" as follows: "The divine manifestation of God, which comes to the flesh to destroy incarnate error;" and on page 589, she defines "Jesus" as, "The highest human corporeal concept of the divine idea, rebuking and destroying error and bringing to light man's immortality."

For Peter to behold Jesus as the Christ in a burst of spiritual illumination, then presently, during the dark hours of the crucifixion, to deny that he ever knew Jesus,

---

* Reprinted from *The Christian Science Journal*, December, 1939, Vol. 57, No. 9.

betrayed a type of weakness which could not be overlooked in a potential church builder. At the last spiritual breakfast on the Galilean shore, Jesus turned to Peter and inquired into the nature of his loyalty. Did Peter's protestations of loyalty ring true? Was this examination preliminary to a momentous decision?

In Jesus' question, "Lovest thou me?" (John 21:15), the word for "love" is the Greek "agapas," which Jesus used at the Last Supper to describe divine Love (John 14:21). In his reply to Jesus, Peter used the Greek word "phileo," which denotes a lesser degree of love than "agapas," and means "to be fond of." The same words for "love" were used in the second question and answer; but the third time Jesus put his question, he used the lower word "phileis," which Peter had used, showing that Jesus recognized Peter's inability to measure up to his Master's spiritual standard of love.

Jesus concluded his examination by a prophetic remark about Peter's latter days. When Peter countered with a question about John's future, Jesus made his historic reply, "If I will that he tarry till I come, what is that to thee?" This use of the word "will" has the significance of "decree" or "ordain," and not even boiling oil could break that decree of Christ Jesus for John so long as John was faithful. Jesus here forecast his revelation to John on Patmos. The decision had been made, and it was

John and not Peter who was ordained to be the recorder of Jesus' prophetic words about the Church.

The Scriptures record frequent covenants between God and man. These covenants are of two types. The prophetic type, such as the coming of the Messiah and of the promised Comforter, were made imperative and unconditional. Another type of covenant is exemplified in the Fifth Commandment of the Mosaic Decalogue in which long life is made conditional upon man's obedience to his father and mother. The opening verse of the Ninety-first Psalm contains a promise which is conditional upon man's attitude toward God. Thus we see that the Bible makes reward conditional upon man's obedience to God's covenant, or upon his measuring up to the divine standard.

As it is with man, so it is with the church, for in Revelation 2:5 and 7, a condition is made for the first of the seven churches, the condition being that unless that church should repent and do the first works, its candlestick would be removed out of its place. In recording Jesus' prophetic words about the seven churches in the opening chapters of the book of Revelation, a description is given of the nature and works of the seven churches, seven being a symbol of completeness or wholeness (1900 Message, p. 14). These seven churches are described as seven golden candlesticks, with one in the midst of them "like unto the Son of man" (Rev. 1:12–13), which is the Christ

(John 8:28). There are also seven stars designated as "the angels of the seven churches" (Rev. 1:20). Mrs. Eddy says, "Spiritual teaching must always be by symbols" (Science and Health, p. 575). The testimony of God is largely committed to these seven churches, and further symbolism shows that they are destined to vanquish seven phases of human error.

The purpose or mission of the Church was attested by Jesus' declaration, "The gates of hell shall not prevail against it." Thus Jesus proclaimed the Church of Christ to be a spiritual idea which would provide a full and complete remedy for sin or hell. It is not difficult to see that such a church — the Church Triumphant — must be spiritually discerned before it could be humanly expressed.

As we have learned from Jesus' words, the province of the Church is to challenge and destroy sin, and Mrs. Eddy helps us to understand the significance of that challenge when she says (Retrospection and Introspection, p. 67), "Sin existed as a false claim before the human concept of sin was formed." That is to say, original sin antedated the individual or human concept of sin. Mrs. Eddy concludes, therefore, that sin or the lie is "collective as well as individual" (*ibid.*, p. 67). Moreover, Jesus' mission, according to Mrs. Eddy, "was both individual and collective" (Science and Health, p. 18). The Church of Christ, because of its membership, is a collective idea, and its province is to challenge the claim of original sin. The mission of the Church therefore prevents original sin from separating God and man, and renders obsolete the belief of a fallen man. So this collective challenge to and destruction of collective sin establishes man's unity or at-one-ment with God, through Christ; and that, according to Webster, is the true sense of atonement.

As we approach the individual side of the problem, we learn from Paul that we must work out our own salvation, meaning thereby salvation from sin, disease, and death. As the Way-shower to individual salvation, Christ Jesus made his healing works "an outward and visible sign of an inward and spiritual grace, which is necessary to the achievement of salvation." That, according to Webster, is the true sense of sacrament.

The last chapter in Science and Health, entitled "Fruitage," contains a hundred pages of testimonies by those who have been healed or regenerated by reading that book. In this way, the Christian Science textbook brings the true sense of sacrament to those who have experienced its healing grace. Each one must achieve his individual salvation through the true sense of sacrament, while at the same time he must join the church and unite with other church members in making a collective challenge to original sin by what is known as the atonement.

There can be no church without sacraments or acts of

consecration sanctioned by Christ Jesus, and these sacraments must be vital and living.   Accordingly, Mrs. Eddy called a meeting of her followers, "To organize a church designed to commemorate the word and works of our Master, which should reinstate primitive Christianity and its lost element of healing" (Manual, p. 17).   In this way she hoped to make the Church itself a vital sacrament in its challenge to sin, instead of a mouthpiece for rites and ceremonies.

Let us here recapitulate some of the steps in church organization already noted in previous chapters.   The first step took place on April 12, 1879 (*ibid.*, p. 17), and a charter was secured in August of that year in the name of "Church of Christ, Scientist."   Mrs. Eddy was the first Pastor of this Church, and she was subsequently ordained in the year 1881 (*ibid.*, p. 18).

Mrs. Eddy learned presently that the infant Church was being hampered in its challenge to sin and disease by its material organization.   In order to make its challenge to sin effectual, the Church seen in prophetic vision must be above the plane of the error it was destined to eradicate. Having clarified the problem to that degree, Mrs. Eddy disorganized her Church on December 2, 1889, about ten years after its inception.   She retained its name and also its charter; for just as the copyright to Science and Health protects our textbook from infringement, so the church charter protects the name of that early Church from improper use.

After the Church was disorganized, regular services were held as before, and the church officers continued to function by common consent as representatives of the congregation. Thus freed from material limitations, the Church prospered wonderfully; but it had lost the legal right to hold property or to erect a church building. With the steady growth of the congregation, there was an ever-increasing need for a church home, and legal minds counseled a reorganization of the Church as the only way out of the dilemma. Fully aware of its consequences, Mrs. Eddy opposed a reorganization. But, having led her students in the right direction as far as they would go, she finally waived her opposition to their demands, and selected twelve of her students to meet on August 29, 1892, with instructions from her to reorganize the Church.

For nearly three years Mrs. Eddy had been searching for the right solution of this church problem in the realm of Spirit, where all things are possible with God. It was not until she waived her opposition to a material organization that the answer to her prayer came through the discovery of a Massachusetts law which provides that "deacons, church wardens, or other similar officers of churches" can hold property in trust for the benefit of the church, and that such officers shall "be deemed bodies corporate."

With the discovery of that law, Mrs. Eddy acted promptly in accordance with its provisions, and issued a deed of trust to four of her students, who were among the twelve whom she had chosen to reorganize the Church. According to this deed of trust, her trustees could hold title to all church property. This new trust deed was read at the meeting called for August 29, 1892, and instead of reorganizing the Church, the meeting voted to approve the new trust deed. It was duly recorded at the Registry of Deeds in Boston, September 2, 1892 (Miscellany, p. 55, and Manual, p. 135). One of the provisions of the trust deed was that the "church shall be styled 'The First Church of Christ, Scientist'." In effect, the deed might be regarded as a new charter, because it gave a new or revised name to the Church.

The congregation, which had been holding services for nearly three years without an organization, now had a self-perpetuating Board of Directors who had the legal right to hold property as trustees for the Church. The much-needed church building could now be erected, and the new Board of Directors was prompt in issuing an initial call for subscriptions to the church building fund.

After the Board of Directors had been functioning in office for about three weeks, Mrs. Eddy asked the same twelve students to meet again on September 23, 1892, and to vote themselves "First Members" of that Church. That group of twelve First Members again introduced into the problem the semblance of a material organization, but it was only a means to an end, and did not long continue.

The date, September 23, 1892, marks the beginning of the present church membership. The twelve First Members, who were selected to organize the Church, added to their number from time to time, as nominations were made by Mrs. Eddy, and this enlarged group of First Members voted into membership lay members who had made personal application to be admitted. Because the previous church organization had been abandoned in December, 1889, it was not until September 23, 1892, when members were first enrolled in the reorganized Church, that the present Christian Science denomination was permanently founded (Manual, p. 18).

Since then, each newly organized Christian Science Church has been known as a branch of the Boston Church.

The relation between The Mother Church and its branches is described by Jesus as follows: "I am the vine, ye are the branches: He that abideth in me, and I in him, the same bringeth forth much fruit." The spiritual identity of the branch church is found in its life-link with The Mother Church, and that spiritual identity makes it possible for the branch church to bring forth fruit in its successful challenge to sin and disease. The Apostle Paul tells us what kind of fruit is expected of church members by enumerating the nine fruits of the Spirit. They are "love, joy, peace, long-suffering, gentleness, goodness, faith, meekness, temperance: against such there is no law." Being elements of true law, these nine graces of the Spirit are all character builders. They rule out friction, irritation, intolerance, impurity, deceit, personal domination, and discord — all sin.

These fruits of the Spirit also set the standard of true democracy in the fellowship of collective action. Events have proved that under the immediate direction of divine power, national governments, as well as individuals, have been blessed. Whenever the type of government that is under the immediate direction of God is humanly expressed, it begets a truly democratic sense of brotherhood. "The Magna Charta of Christian Science means much," says Mrs. Eddy. She continues, "Essentially democratic, its government is administered by the common consent of the governed, wherein and whereby man governed by his creator is self-governed" (Miscellany, pp. 246, 247).

Personal preaching was continued after Mrs. Eddy retired from the pastorate, but she saw in it certain potential dangers. Turning again to the realm of Spirit, Mrs. Eddy sought patiently and prayerfully for a pastor who could withstand the temptations of priestly office. In answer to her prayers, she ordained "the Bible, and 'Science and Health with Key to the Scriptures,' to be hereafter the only pastor of The Church of Christ, Scientist, throughout our land and in other lands" (Miscellaneous Writings, pp. 313, 314). Since the dedication of The Mother Church edifice in January, 1895, this "divinely authorized" pastor has been preaching for all Christian Science churches throughout the world.

A pastor must have a subject for his sermon, and Mrs. Eddy submitted twenty-six permanent subjects to a Bible Lesson Committee appointed by the Trustees of The Christian Science Publishing Society. The subjects of Sacrament and Atonement were included in the list, and later the subject of Thanksgiving was added. It is the duty of the Bible Lesson Committee to prepare Lesson-Sermons on the subjects selected by Mrs. Eddy, and these Lesson-Sermons are read in all Christian Science churches. The Readers, who are selected by each church, are required to prepare themselves properly for reading the Sunday Lesson-Sermon, "a lesson on which the prosperity of Christian Science largely depends" (Manual, p. 31).

The original purpose of the midweek meetings of the Church was to provide opportunity for discussing the Lesson of the previous Sunday, somewhat like an open forum. The resulting personal bias and controversy, so common to open forums, were finally supplanted by testimonies based on the fruitage of Christian Science healing. This acknowledged the lost element of healing as an essential function of the Church. Nine days after the new pastor was instituted for the Sunday services, Mrs. Eddy wrote concerning the midweek meetings:

Concord, New Hampshire.

January 15, 1895.

"My dear students:

"Make broader your bounds for blessing the people. Have Friday evening meetings to benefit the people. Learn to forget what you should not remember, — viz., self, and live for the good you do. Conduct your meetings by repeating and demonstrating practical Christian Science. Tell what this Science does for yourself, and will do for others. Speak from experience of its Founder, noting her self-sacrifice as the way in Christian Science. Be meek; let your mottoes for these meetings be: *Who shall be least and servant;* and 'Little children, love one another.'

Affectionately yours,

(*Signed*) MARY BAKER EDDY."

This new order for the weekday meetings featured two distinct points. The first is a request to "tell what this Science does for yourself and will do for others." The second is a request to "speak from experience of" Mrs.

Eddy as the one who pointed the way in Christian Science. We all know how uncertain our gropings would be but for the self-sacrifice of our Leader in blazing the way for us. This new order of service brought about the union of the letter and the spirit in the fruitage of Christian Science; and it also joined the messenger to the message in grateful acknowledgment (Miscellaneous Writings, p. 105). The time of meeting was changed from Friday evening to Wednesday evening in June, 1898.

An item of business required of the First Members was to vote the adoption of the various church By-laws which Mrs. Eddy wrote and submitted for their approval. These By-laws were later collated and published in 1895 as our Church Manual. After the Manual took form and began to function in the government of the Church, the First Members adopted a By-law, submitted by Mrs. Eddy, which transferred to the Board of Directors all matters of business, including the adoption of any further By-laws which Mrs. Eddy might submit to them. That action terminated the usefulness of the First Members, and on July 8, 1908, the By-laws relating to First Members, later known as Executive Members, were repealed. This act removed from the Christian Science Church the last vestige of a material organization. The Church Manual administered by the Board of Directors, now increased to five members, constituted the government of the Church, and the Church Triumphant emerged into view! In the language of Mrs. Eddy, "this spiritually organized Church of Christ, Scientist, in Boston, still goes on" (Retrospection and Introspection, pp. 44, 45).

The divine idea of the Church and its mission were clearly outlined by Jesus. These promises were repeated in the symbolism of Revelation. But was the completed temple, the visible idea, and its form of church government ever seen in prophecy? We read in the Scriptures, "The testimony of Jesus is the spirit of prophecy," and his testimony in the eleventh chapter of Revelation describes "the temple of God" and its form of government. "A reed like unto a rod" was presented by the angel to measure the temple, and this rod is explained in the next chapter as a symbol of government, even the government of divine Science. (See Science and Health, p. 565.) Like our Church Manual, this rod governs "the temple of God, and the altar" where sacraments are offered through all of its institutional activities, "and them that worship therein." This symbol of government in the hand of the angel is under the immediate direction or administration of God. In like manner our Church Manual, as well as the teachings of Science and Health, rules our church temple, its sacraments and members, under the immediate direction or administration of God. Such a form of government is neither autocratic nor democratic; it is a pure theocracy, or government by God, and The Mother Church is doubtless the first successful theocracy since the Hebrew commonwealth instituted by Moses.

Mrs. Eddy said to Adam H. Dickey, "I prayed God day and night to show me how to form my Church, and how to go on with it. I understand that He showed me, just as I understand He showed me Christian Science, and no human being ever showed me Christian Science. Then I have no right or desire to change what God has directed me to do, and it remains for the Church to obey it. What has prospered this Church for thirty years will continue to keep it."

The Mother Church is the first appearing of the spiritually organized Church in the fulfillment of prophecy. The corner-stone of our church temple, with its contents, according to Mrs. Eddy, typifies the prophecy of our Master, "Upon this rock I will build my church; and the gates of hell shall not prevail against it." (See Miscellaneous Writings, p. 144.) She says further, that "The First Church of Christ, Scientist, our prayer in stone, will be the prophecy fulfilled, the monument upreared, of Christian Science. It will speak to you of the Mother, and of your hearts' offering to her through whom was revealed to you God's all-power, all-presence, and all-science. . . . Of our first church in Boston, O recording angel! write: God is in the midst of her" (Miscellaneous Writings, p. 141).

Mrs. Eddy has said, "In 1896 it goes without saying, preeminent over ignorance or envy, that Christian Science *is founded by its discoverer*, and built upon the rock of Christ" (*ibid.*, p. 383).

Ira Oscar Knapp

Flavia Stickney Knapp

Bliss Knapp upon graduation from Harvard College.
Courtesy of Longyear Museum and Historical Society.

Bliss Knapp
Courtesy of Longyear Museum and Historical Society.

Bliss and Eloise Mabury Knapp
Courtesy of Longyear Museum and Historical Society.

Shown, from left to right: Irving C. Tomlinson, John W. Reeder, Bliss Knapp and William P. McKenzie.

Courtesy of Longyear Museum and Historical Society.

Ira O. Knapp   William B. Johnson   Joseph Armstrong   Stephen A. Chase

Directors of Mary Baker G. Eddy's Church in 1895.

The Christian Science Board of Directors in 1892
Shown, from left to right: Ira O. Knapp, William B.
Johnson, Joseph Armstrong, and Stephen A. Chase.

T has ever been a peculiarity of human nature to relegate prophecy and prophets to the past. It is as much a truism that a prophet is not without honor save in his own age and generation, as that he is not without honor save in his own country. When the great Prophet of Nazareth appeared on the world's arena, teaching as no prophet had taught before him and proving the efficacy of his teaching by the performance of works that no prophet had performed before him, his age and generation rejected him and his teachings, and refused to believe in the divinity of his works, although compelled to admit that they were wonderful and above all human understanding.

It was easy for that age and generation to believe that Moses, Elijah, and many others who had flourished in previous times, were prophets. Their teachings were unquestionably accepted by the Jews as of divine authority. But to believe that there was actually then amongst them a prophet greater than any who had preceded him was more than the blindness of that age and generation was ready for. Only a few would believe and accept. Yet Jesus' coming had long and repeatedly been foretold, and a Messianic appearing was generally expected among the Jews,—the people who, more than any other, refused to receive him.

A second-coming is as clearly prophesied as was the first coming. The Old Testament writers foretold it, Jesus plainly prophesied it, and the apostles reiterated these prophecies. The only question among believers in the Bible has been as to the time and manner of the coming. In respect to this there has been, and yet is, much disputation, speculation, and controversy. A personal coming is generally believed in, and the only personality that will at present meet the general expectancy of Christendom is the identical personality of Jesus as he appeared nineteen hundred years ago.

Only, as yet, a comparatively small part of mankind are ready to accept the larger coming comprehended in a re-establishment of the religious régime which Jesus inaugurated. This small part of mankind are satisfied that the second-coming has commenced and is now manifesting itself

Detail of the galley proof intended for the *Christian Science Journal*, "Editor's Table" by Judge Septimus J. Hanna.

XI

THE IMPORTANCE OF CHURCH MEMBERSHIP

CHAPTER XI

———————————*———————————

* The Importance of Church Membership

WHY is it important to be a church member? One way to answer such a question is to learn what is involved. We know that Christian Science is a religion of works, and that it does benefit those who invoke its protection. The nature of its benefits is shown by the experience of the beggar who asked the apostles Peter and John for alms as they were about to enter the temple. This man had been lame from birth, but instead of giving him money, Peter commanded him in the name of Jesus Christ to stand on his feet and walk. His healing was immediate, and, knowing that God alone could produce such a miracle, he went into the temple with the apostles, glorifying God. Such is the fruitage of divine power, and its natural association with the church.

Christian healing stimulates the desire to look into the realm of Spirit; it invites one to explore its divine possi-

———————————

* Reprinted from the *Christian Science Sentinel*, March 2, 1946, Vol. 48, No. 9.

bilities and to grasp its real significance. Christian healing holds the key to the problem of salvation.

Knowing that all must work out their individual salvation, each one of us must become aware of his present shortcomings. The discipline of family life is helpful when it chastens pride and selfishness and marks the difference between right and wrong; it is helpful in character building when it develops respect, affection, and unity in the home. When one unites with the family of church members, he finds the same discipline which heightens the desire to do right. Church membership is a training school for developing the graces of the Spirit in our passage from sense to Soul.

In the prophetic pages of the book of Revelation we find a record of the varied problems which confront the church and its members, and a warning to overcome these errors. Nothing is left to the imagination as to what is required of a church member. This should rouse our interest, because what the Revelator writes about the seven churches of Asia is prophetic of the church of today. Significantly enough, the first requirement for a church and its members is the preservation of their early enthusiasm, such as the beggar manifested when he was healed.

The Revelator's first message was addressed to the church of Ephesus. From his amplified statement we learn that this church took its stand against evil and labored patiently to overcome it; but, although the church did not faint in well-doing, it lost its early enthusiasm, which he calls its first love. The warning which follows, implies that the loss of that first love must be repented of until the first works can be repeated, because life itself is conditional upon keeping aglow that first love.

But for such a warning, we today might not know how important to this spiritual warfare is the need to preserve our first love. Jesus sounded the same warning when he said (Matt. 24:12), "Because iniquity shall abound, the love of many shall wax cold." But he promised that those who could endure to the end of the error would be saved. And the Revelator also promised that they would abide in the paradise which God has prepared for those who are faithful unto the end.

It is to be regretted that sometimes a church member grows spiritually dull, but now that we have the warning as to its consequences, let us learn what we must do to keep our spiritual light burning brightly. The teachings of Mary Baker Eddy make it clear that the only restorative for spiritual sense is divine Love. When spiritual sense actuates one's thinking, the individual and the church can repeat the works of the early apostles in healing the ills of the flesh. The necessity of the church member is therefore to maintain the clarity of his spiritual sense, by which his healing power becomes spontaneous.

The Revelator sounds the warning that unless its first love is maintained by the church, its candlestick or spiritual light will be removed from its place. Only error could cloud one's spiritual sense, and repentance is the remedy. When sorrow for wrongdoing goes deep enough, there will be reformation. The lesson must be learned that the glow of spiritual sense, which is our first love, must be kept clear at all times, and that becomes the paramount obligation of a church member. It requires self-discipline, stemming from the love to do right in obedience to Principle.

The spiritual progress of a church is commensurate with the spiritual progress of its members. When new members are taken into the church, their zeal, loyalty, and good works should strengthen and advance its purpose. If some fall short of the spiritual requirements and lose the desire for self-discipline, "these," according to Jesus, "have no root, which for a while believe, and in time of temptation fall away" (Luke 8:13). Thus it is that some members who are lacking in self-discipline are shaken out of their place.

Perhaps the most frequent stumbling block to spiritual progress is personality. One may absent himself from church services simply because another member's personality is offensive to him. Thus he is giving power to another, who may be totally unaware of the condition, to rule him out of his place in the temple. If personal sense gets offended or hurt, let us remember that the restoration of spiritual sense contains the remedy for such a belief of minds many. Take the case of Joshua and his band, when they laid siege to Jericho. As they marched around the city, they all had to shout together; they had to be of one Mind; and because they were of one Mind, the walls fell and the city was captured. But suppose some member of the company had complained to Joshua that a fellow member irritated him so much that he could no longer walk with him. Such a mental state would have hindered the demonstration of the one Mind. Self-will must be put down in order for one to be a good church member.

Mrs. Eddy has told us how we can overcome this stumbling block of personality by taking a leaf from the ministry of Christ Jesus. John the Baptist prophesied that the Messiah or Christ would open his ministry bearing a fan in hand, and that the purpose of this fan would be to purge the threshing floor by separating the chaff from the wheat. Jesus knew how to look into a human personality and separate the good traits from the bad, like winnowing a threshing floor. In like manner, "the Science of Christianity comes with fan in hand to separate the chaff from the wheat" (Science and Health, p. 466). We must therefore approach this problem of personality scientifically with fan in hand, for this fan symbolizes the power of Christ to separate error from truth. So when we, as church members, have to deal with the question of personalities, let us be sure that we are governed by the Christ, Truth.

In answering the question, "What are spirits and souls?" Mrs. Eddy says (Science and Health, p. 466), "To human belief they are personalities constituted of mind and matter, life and death, truth and error, good and evil; but these contrasting pairs of terms represent contraries, as Christian Science reveals, which neither dwell together nor assimilate." Thus the Science of Christianity separates the error or chaff from the individual, because these contrasting elements never mix or blend.

Taking in hand his fan, which symbolizes the Science of Christ's coming, the church member can see his associates as they really are — pure, perfect, and harmonious. With such associates he can reflect the one Mind and bring out harmony in himself and in the church. Such is the reward of a restored spiritual sense under self-discipline. Even if this result is bought with a price, it is worth all the effort we put into it.

Turning next to the church in Smyrna, we find a different type of problem. Here the searchlight is brought to bear upon the loyalty of its members to the teachings of the church. Suppose, for example, a church member has an unsolved problem, and he is physically ill. His loyalty is being tested. Shall he hold to a radical reliance on God according to the teachings of his textbooks? We read that Asa, while king of Israel, was diseased in his feet, and when he turned to the physicians instead of to God, he died.

Immortality is a teaching of the Christian church, and church members should prepare themselves for immortality by solving, in so far as they are able, their own problems now. One becomes a stronger church member as he proves his ability to stand on his own foundation and not lean on the support of others. Loyal to the teachings of Christian Science, the church members look for healing in no other direction. They maintain the clarity of their spiritual sense through self-discipline and adherence to Principle; and because of their fidelity to that Principle, they gain the crown of life.

The Revelator addressed his third admonition to the church in Pergamos with a warning against mental occultism or animal magnetism. St. Paul helps us to understand this mental occultism by describing the warfare between the flesh and the Spirit, and he wrote so explicitly about the weapons of that warfare that it is a vital part of church activity for Christians to learn how to cope with evil's claims. The church difficulty in Pergamos was that some of the church members were still holding to the teachings of Balaam, and they were seducing the children of Israel to commit fornication and to worship idols before the throne of Satan. But other members were faithful to the true God, and the promise to them was that they would be fed with "hidden manna" or spiritual meat, and in that regeneration they would receive a new name.

That is a fairly accurate picture of what is going on in the world today. Obedience to the moral law is being jeopardized. But what if Balaam did teach Balak how to corrupt the Israelites, did not Moses lead the chosen people out of Egyptian darkness by the strength of the moral law? Just when the moral law seems to be most profaned, as at the present time, we find in the writings of our Leader the same "hidden manna" or spiritual meat which enables the individual to avoid deviation from moral rectitude, or sound thinking. It is that spiritual regeneration which gives us the new name of Christian Scientist.

Moses, the lawgiver, was the first man in Bible history to employ the power of God to overcome the claims of the magicians and to heal leprosy and serpent bites. To those who ask how Moses accomplished such healing, and how Christian healing is accomplished today, we respond in Mrs. Eddy's words (Science and Health, p. 72), "Not personal intercommunion but divine law is the communicator of truth, health, and harmony to earth and humanity." Moses being the first one to know the divine law, he was the first one, according to the Bible, to employ the power of God to heal sin, disease, and sorcery by its means.

Jesus summarized the Ten Commandments, representing the law as understood by Moses, into two great commandments, namely, "Thou shalt love the Lord thy God," and, "Thou shalt love thy neighbour as thyself" (Mark 12:30, 31). When our roots go deep enough in obedience to these two great commandments and the law of God they proclaim, we can withstand the wiles of mental occultism or animal magnetism. We can establish our protection from the problems which beset the church in Pergamos. Only as we protect ourselves from fornication and idolatry can we demonstrate the holiness of divine power which gives us the right to the new name of Christian Scientist.

We have considered three church problems which must be solved by the church members: the need of maintaining spiritual clarity through self-discipline; the need of absolute loyalty to the teachings of the church; and the need of obedience to the moral law to the point of being regenerated or renamed in Christian Science. Name and nature being much the same thing, this new name designates what Jesus meant when he told Nicodemus that he must be born again; it is the new birth into spiritual regeneration. Definitely these are three essential steps in our problem of salvation, and they characterize worthiness for, as well as the importance of, church membership. If one sees the vastness of its opportunities, he will never feel that he has outgrown the benefits of church membership.

Did we but realize what the church has in store for us, we would be eager to take our fan in hand and enter the threshing floor as we would the schoolroom, and learn how to separate fable from fact.   We would be eager to accept rebuke and correction lovingly, and be able to say with the Master (Luke 22:42), "Not my will, but thine, be done."   Above all, we would learn the true meaning of theocratic government as it is expressed in the Manual of The Mother Church.

XII

THE WOMAN

CHAPTER XII

∗

The Woman

CHRIST JESUS frequently spoke in parables, and one of his most distinctive parables is the following: "The kingdom of heaven is like unto leaven, which a woman took, and hid in three measures of meal, till the whole was leavened." This he said in fulfilling the prophecy, "I will open my mouth in parables; I will utter things which have been kept secret from the foundation of the world" (Matt. 13:33, 35). The fact that this parable about the Woman was "kept secret from the foundation of the world," implies that she was no ordinary woman and that her mission must be unique.

This parable completely upset the accepted symbolism of the Bible commentators. To them, a woman symbolizes something out of place, religiously, and Jezebel is her type. When Elijah incurred the wrath of this awful queen, Jezebel, he fled for his life. Being the patroness of false prophets, she called herself a prophetess; and some centuries later she reappeared in the book of Revelation as a woman who is suffered to teach her sorceries to the church at Thyatira.   So, the Babylonish phase of an apostate church is symbolized by an unchaste woman.

Jezebel is a type or symbol, because she exemplifies qualities or characteristics common to a number of individuals.   But this new Woman in Jesus' parable is not typical of any individual hitherto known, because she has been "kept secret from the foundation of the world." Moreover, her mission is likewise unique, because she is destined to hide a new kind of leaven in three measures of meal, till the whole is leavened.

I say a new kind of leaven, because leaven as a symbolic or typical substance, is used in the Old Testament in an evil sense.   In fact this new leaven, according to the commentators, does violence to the meaning fixed by Jesus himself, when he warns us to "beware of the leaven of the Pharisees and of the Sadducees," by which is meant their false doctrines (Matt. 16:6,12). This new Gospel is expected to convert the whole world by a leavening process, which is a new and different method from that which is expressed in the parable of the "Wheat and the Tares." Instead of sowing seed, the new order is to mix leaven with the meal, or three modes of thought, which Mrs. Eddy interprets as Science, Theology, and Medicine, until the whole is irresistibly leavened or transformed.

Mrs. Eddy describes the leaven referred to in this parable as "the spiritual leaven" which "signifies the Science of Christ and its spiritual interpretation, — an inference far above the merely ecclesiastical and formal applications of the illustration" (Science and Health, p. 118). She also says that this parable foretells "the second appearing in the flesh of the Christ, Truth, hidden in sacred secrecy from the visible world" (*ibid.*). The first appearing of Christ came in the flesh, for Jesus said, "a spirit hath not flesh and bones, as ye see me have" (Luke 24:39). Then, according to Mrs. Eddy, the second appearing of Christ in the flesh would come through this Woman whose mission has been known to God "from the foundation of the world," even as Jesus' mission was known. Her place, like his, being unique, it would have to be made known in creation, as recorded in the first chapter of Genesis. She would not be a type or a symbol of any other person or event; she is the original Woman, even as Mrs. Eddy refers to Jesus as the original man (*ibid.*, p. 286).

Inasmuch as "the spiritual leaven signifies the Science of Christ," our search for this Science would naturally lead us to investigate "Science and Health with Key to the Scriptures." And what of this book? The prophet Ezekiel tells about "a roll of a book" which, when eaten, would be "in my mouth as honey for sweetness" (Ezek. 2:9, 3:3). Only in prophetic vision could the book be seen and the sweetness of its taste be noted. Ezekiel's contemporary, Daniel, records another glimpse of this book. But

Daniel was required, at God's command, to "shut up the words, and seal the book, even to the time of the end" (Dan. 12:4). So this book must be kept "in sacred secrecy" until "the time of the end," when the seals would be unloosed.

In the book of Revelation, written several centuries later, we learn more about this book which was "sealed with seven seals" (Rev. 5:10). There it is recorded that "no man in heaven, nor in earth, neither under the earth, was able to open the book, neither to look thereon" (*ibid.*, 5:3). The opening of this book was a problem beyond the power of any man to solve. Only "the Lion of the tribe of Juda, the Root of David," could unseal the book. Christ Jesus referred to himself as "the root and the offspring of David" (*ibid.*, 22:16), which bespeaks his dual nature of the unseen and the seen, and the Root is Christ. Although no man, not even Jesus, could unseal the book, his Root or Christ could unseal it. Consequently the Lamb of God, which is the Christ, "came and took the book out of the right hand of him that sat upon the throne" (*ibid.*, 5:7).

The divine origin of this book is evidenced by the fact that it is held in the right hand of God, and only the Lamb could take it out of His hand. This account is recorded in the fifth chapter of Revelation. Since the book was sevensealed, the next four chapters in Revelation describe the seals, and their final destruction by the Lamb. Then comes the tenth chapter with "the little book" opened for all to read and understand. The lesson to be learned is that the seals are only hidden or unsolved problems of evil which have found lodgment in "Science, Theology, and Medicine." Then in God's own time, the new leaven contained in "the little book," and prepared "from the foundation of the world," must be planted in those three modes of thought by the original Woman, whose place and destiny are unique. Then let no one flippantly remark that any one who was listening could have written "the little book," or that it could possibly be a plagiarism of any other work.

Daniel saw in prophetic vision just when we might expect the advent of this book which he had sealed, and he described it as a period ending with "a time, times, and an half" (Dan. 12:7), or 1260 days (Rev. 11:3). We may not understand what that means, but Mrs. Eddy says, "It is authentically said that one expositor of Daniel's dates fixed the year 1866 or 1867 for the return of Christ — the return of the spiritual idea to the material earth or antipode of heaven. It is a marked coincidence that those dates were the first two years of my discovery of Christian Science" (Miscellany, p. 181). Again she writes, "Some modern exegesis on the prophetic Scriptures cites 1875 as the year of the second coming of Christ. In that year the Christian Science textbook, 'Science and Health with Key to the Scriptures,' was first published" (1900 Message, p. 6).

There were two more dates in Daniel's calculations, 1290 and 1335, making three prophetic dates in all. If the first one, 1260, points to the year in which Christian Science was discovered, and this fact has Mrs. Eddy's approval, it is significant that the second date, 1290, points to the year 1896, when our Church Manual was well launched, and when Mrs. Eddy said of it, "eternity awaits our Church Manual" (Miscellany, p. 230).

Mrs. Eddy has claimed three titles, — Discoverer and Founder of Christian Science, and Leader of the movement. According to Daniel's dates, the year 1866 marks the time for the discovery; thirty years later, or 1896, marks the time for the founding of Christian Science, inasmuch as the Church Manual provides for the institutional activities of Mrs. Eddy's Church. Then Daniel says, "Blessed is he that waiteth and cometh to the" (Dan. 12:12) last named date, which is 1335. That brings us to about the year 1940 or 1941, when we may expect the title of Leader to be fully acknowledged. The prophesied blessing may be the joy that comes to one who recognizes the "visible idea" which has been kept secret "from the foundation of the world."

All this may help to explain something which we may

have forgotten. Let us turn back the pages of history to the fifth annual meeting of The National Christian Scientist Association, which was held in New York City on May 27, 1890. One of the principal speakers at that meeting was Dr. E. J. Foster Eddy, and among other things, he said, "The Leader whom God has chosen to present this Truth to the world, to deliver His people, is going before us." Also he said, "In union of thought and purpose is strength."

Another speaker at the same meeting was Mrs. Augusta E. Stetson. Referring to the battle between Truth and error, she said, "Jesus the Christ worked out the problem, and left the 'Way' for all who would follow Him. In this century, it is a woman, Rev. Mary B. G. Eddy, to whom the Truth of Being — her risen Lord — has been revealed; . . . She, as God's interpreter, has heralded the power of Omnipotent Mind" (*The Christian .Science Journal*, Vol. VIII, pp. 141 and 148).

In the next number of the *Journal*, August, 1890, Mrs. Eddy said, "The late articles referring to me in July issue of the Journal, contain presentiments that I object to having uttered or written now in regard to myself. . . . It is my impression that at least a half century will pass away before man is permitted to render his public verdict on some of the momentous questions that are now agitating the world." From this it is clear that Mrs. Eddy did not wish much to be said *publicly* regarding her leadership until about the year 1940. Mrs. Eddy once said, "The right thing, done at the wrong time, is no longer the right thing" (Powell).

In her address to that same meeting, in which Mrs. Eddy recommended that The National Christian Scientist Association should disorganize, she said, "I once thought that in unity was human strength; but have grown to know that human strength is weakness, — that in unity with divine might alone is power and peace" (*The Christian Science Journal*, Vol. VIII, p. 140).

Sometime during the year 1898, Judge Septimus J. Hanna, who was then serving as First Reader of The Mother Church, and editor of the periodicals, was led to give special attention to the 53rd and 54th chapters of the book of Isaiah. It was revealed to him that the 54th chapter is as distinctly a prophecy of Mrs. Eddy as the 53rd chapter is a prophecy of Jesus. As he pondered this unfolding, he decided to write an editorial embodying his views. When the editorial was set up in galley proof, the courtesy of showing it to Mrs. Eddy before publication brought it to her attention.

The editorial struck a responsive chord in Mrs. Eddy's thought, for it reminded her of a vision which had come to her twenty-one years before, when the first revolt had taken place in her Church, leaving her with but one or two loyal students, and when she was without salary or funds. In that darkest hour, the people scorned her teachings, and even those whom she had raised from the dream of death shunned her in the street. Then came to her in vision that remarkable utterance, addressed to the "Daughter of Zion," which said, "She shall sit under her own vine and fig tree, and all peoples shall hear her gladly." This came back to her when she read Judge Hanna's editorial, and she recommended its publication with this addition: "We know there is but one God, one Christ Jesus, and one mother of Jesus. But we deem it no infringement to regard the fulfilment of Scripture as indicated at the present period, and named therein, a self-evident proof thereof — not confined to personality but the works which declare the Word."

Further correspondence with Mrs. Eddy about that editorial brought out her desire to have it made a leader in *The Christian Science Journal* for greater publicity. Then she uttered a note of caution to the effect that, although the editorial was perfectly true, and infinite Love had inspired Judge Hanna to write it, nevertheless the time had not yet come to publish it. So it was filed away for future use.

Shortly after Judge Hanna's editorial on the 54th chapter of Isaiah was written and had received Mrs. Eddy's emphatic approval, one of her students brought a lawsuit against Mrs. Eddy for the purpose of forcing her to testify in open court in regard to her place in Bible prophecy. That which provoked the suit was Mrs. Eddy's Communion Message to The Mother Church for June 4, 1899, in which she made certain statements about the Babylonish woman (Miscellany, p. 124). Mrs. Josephine C. Woodbury personalized those statements, and decided they were intended for herself. A suit for libel against Mrs. Eddy was brought by Mrs. Woodbury in the Massachusetts Superior Court for the sum of $150,000. Mrs. Woodbury filed a similar suit for libel against Mrs. Eddy at the same time in the United States Circuit Court, sitting at Concord, New Hampshire, in order to compel Mrs. Eddy to appear in court as a witness, either in Boston or in Concord.

The Bill of Complaint contained about fifteen thousand words asserting, among other things, that Mrs. Eddy claimed to be the Woman in the Apocalypse, and that she also claimed Science and Health to be inspired. This brings to mind Jesus' experience with a similar problem. "A man with an unclean spirit" recognized him, and called him "the Holy one of God." Jesus promptly rebuked the man for uttering that truth, because the remark was made with a devilish motive (Mark 1:25). Because the motive which induced this suit for libel was no less devilish, the presiding judge was asked by Mrs. Eddy's own lawyers to strike out of the Bill of Complaint those perfectly true assertions about Mrs. Eddy and her book, and it was so ordered by the Court.

The amended Bill of Complaint was still unsatisfactory, however, and a second demurrer suit was filed and won by Mrs. Eddy's lawyers, which narrowed the case down to the sole issue as to whether Mrs. Eddy's reference to the Babylonish woman in her Communion Message meant any specific woman. Meanwhile Mrs. Woodbury was sued for contempt of Court, and paid a fifty dollar fine, so that the main issue did not actually come to trial until the spring of 1901.

After presenting several witnesses, the plaintiff's lawyer admitted in court that he was unable to prove what the members of the congregation might have believed when they heard Mrs. Eddy's Communion Message read in church. That narrowed his case down to the sole issue as to what Mrs. Eddy had in mind when she wrote those statements about the Babylonish woman. After four days of testimony by witnesses, the prosecution turned the case over to the defense. Mrs. Eddy's lawyers then claimed that the plaintiff had failed to prove that the defendant was at all personal in her reference to the Babylonish woman, because it was a purely impersonal reference, and was used to describe a well-known type of sin. Also they added that Mrs. Woodbury had not denied the illegiti-

macy of her third child. Without presenting a single witness for the defense, Mrs. Eddy's lawyers then asked the
judge to render a verdict for the defendant. The jury was
thereupon instructed to render a verdict for the defendant,
and the case was finished.

In the face of this seeming victory, the Woodbury trial
left some pretty deep scars. Many of the church members
were bewildered, and their mental attitude was comparable to that of some of the disciples after the crucifixion
of Jesus. Unable to recognize him after his resurrection,
two of his followers said to Jesus, "we trusted that it had
been he which should have redeemed Israel" (Luke
24:21). But Jesus rebuked them for so quickly distrusting
prophecy, and he exclaimed, "O fools and slow of heart
to believe all that the prophets have spoken" (*ibid.*, v. 25).
And so the Woodbury trial generated a crop of skeptics
who began to evolve two very troublesome by-products,
which have kept many Christian Scientists wandering
in the wilderness ever since.

One of those by-products was the plot to drive a wedge
between Mrs. Eddy and the Science she discovered. While
accepting Christian Science as the promised Comforter,
some of the church members began to question Mrs.
Eddy's true status concerning this Science. It was only
one more step for them to regard her as only a type or
symbol of "feminine thought," even as Jezebel is another

type of "feminine thought." They were afraid to concede that Mrs. Eddy ever had a place in Bible prophecy such as Judge Hanna had expressed in his editorial, and which Mrs. Eddy had approved. Thus the wedge began to grow into the other by-product of the Woodbury trial which seduced people into believing that anyone who was listening for God's voice could have discovered Christian Science, and that they could claim equality with Mary Baker Eddy and even with Christ Jesus. The facts that Jesus is "the only begotten Son," and that the woman had been "kept secret from the foundation of the world," were rejected by them.

Jesus knew how an inflated ego would cause some to aspire to the office of Christ, and he sounded the warning, "If any man shall say unto you, Lo, here is Christ, or there; believe it not. For there shall arise false Christs, and false prophets, and shall shew great signs and wonders; insomuch that, if it were possible, they shall deceive the very elect" (Matt. 24:23–24). Now our great Master was not an alarmist, but this problem of deception was a decided challenge. And now we have the remedy. It is expressed quite simply. The church in Thyatira, as reported in the second chapter of Revelation, is where Jezebel was suffered to teach her method of seducing members with her sensuous wiles, and those who were made immune to that form of deception were promised "the morning star" (Rev. 2:28).

What is there about this "morning star" which provides the remedy for the Babylonish woman? We are reminded that the angel of Jesus Christ appeared to the apostle John on the island of Patmos and gave him the book of Revelation. In the concluding chapter of that book, there is the following record which contains the answer to our question: "I Jesus have sent mine angel to testify unto you these things in the churches. I am the root and the off-spring of David, and the bright and morning star" (Rev. 22:16). So Jesus acknowledged himself to be "the morning star," and in his message to the church in Thyatira, he gave "the morning star" as the remedy for that type of an apostate church.

It was "the morning star" which guided the Wisemen of the East to seek the promised Messiah, and they found him in Bethlehem of Judea. The angel of this same Messiah, or Christ, provided the remedy for all deception in four assignments which must be carried out by the Woman, who was crowned with twelve stars. One assignment, as recorded in the book of Revelation, was that her child must rule all nations and peoples "imperatively, absolutely, finally—with divine Science," the promised Comforter (Science and Health, p. 565). Another assignment for this Woman, God-crowned, was to produce "the little book," which had from the time of Daniel been sealed with seven seals. A third assignment was to establish the church universal and triumphant. And a fourth assignment was to reveal the fourth side of the Holy City, which is another way of saying that Christian Science would be the complete, or final revelation of truth.

As a convincing proof that God Himself gave this revelation, containing these four assignments for the Woman to accomplish (Rev. 1:1), we have this testimony, "For I testify unto every man that heareth the words of the prophecy of this book, If any man shall add unto these things, God shall add unto him the plagues that are written in this book: And if any man shall take away from the words of the book of this prophecy, God shall take away his part out of the book of life, and out of the holy city, and from the things which are written in this book" (Rev. 22:18,19). It is "the morning star" which has revealed the remedy for every type of deception, and the Woman whom God has appointed and anointed has made the remedy demonstrable and practical. Then in the words of Jesus, "whoso readeth, let him understand" (Matt. 24:15). And "What God knows, He also predestinates; and it must be fulfilled" (No and Yes, p. 37).

XIII

HOW DIVINITY REACHES HUMANITY

CHAPTER XIII

✳

How Divinity Reaches Humanity

In the Glossary to Science and Health, Mrs. Eddy gives the spiritual sense of certain Bible terms which, she says, "is also their original meaning." In that chapter, she concludes a lengthy definition of the divine Mind as follows: "Deity, which outlines but is not outlined." That definition has been accepted by some readers to mean that one should avoid outlining his career if he wishes to progress in Christian Science. However, the very refusal to shape one's course implies a wrong concept of Deity, and it works untold mischief in one's personal affairs.

A certain young man, drilled in the theory that one should never outline his course of action in Christian Science, became as unstable as water. His disbelief in outlining caused him to drift from one task to another until that gifted musician was forced into menial labor to avoid starvation. When he refused to outline or plan his course, the self-discipline required of one whose purpose is to gain artistic merit, came to a stop. Science and Health teaches that "The Christian Scientist wisely shapes his course, and

is honest and consistent in following the leadings of divine
Mind." (Science and Health, p. 458).

Then how can we reconcile that statement with the fact
that the divine Mind also "outlines but is not outlined?"
An outline marks the outer limits of an object or figure; it
is a plan or system of action. A limitless God must be
above and beyond all limits. He can never be outlined
nor placed within contours. Mrs. Eddy says, "We can
have but one Mind, if that one is infinite." (Science and
Health, p. 469).

A limited sense of the divine providence which resulted
in famine, drove the Hebrews into Egyptian bondage. To
the degree that they learned from Moses how to obey the
great I AM, and His freedom from limits, their emancipa-
tion from human bondage began. Instead of drifting
aimlessly, those Hebrews had to learn how to do by nature
the things contained in the law. It was a schooling in
self-discipline. Then they were ready to receive the Ten
Commandments, by which divinity reaches humanity.
Science and Health says, "Not personal intercommunion
but divine law is the communicator of truth, health, and
harmony to earth and humanity." (p. 72).

Then how is it that God, who is devoid of limits, can
outline? Does that imply that Deity can place limits upon
certain things? Is it a contradiction to say that the divine
Mind "outlines but is not outlined?" Here is Mrs. Eddy's

answer: "In this volume of mine there are no contradictory statements, — at least none which are apparent to those who understand its propositions well enough to pass judgment upon them." (Science and Health, p. 345). As one gains a higher concept of divine Science, that which he once believed to be a contradiction will disappear. To the degree that "Moses advanced a nation to the worship of God in Spirit instead of matter" (Science and Health, p. 200), what happened? Their limitations began to disappear humanly, until their personal possessions, such as their clothing, no longer disintegrated during their forty years in the wilderness. That was an object-lesson to show how divinity reaches humanity through the operation of divine law; and the outlining is always entirely within the human realm.

The Immaculate Conception is an object-lesson of how Deity can outline, without being outlined. Concerning that, Mrs. Eddy writes, "Jesus' personality in the flesh, so far as material sense could discern it, was like that of other men; but Science exchanges this human concept of Jesus for the divine ideal, his spiritual individuality that reflected the Immanuel, or 'God with us.' This God was not outlined. He was too mighty for that." (Miscellaneous Writings, p. 103). To material sense, Jesus was like other men, but in the transition from sense to Soul, he can be recognized as the divine ideal. Mrs. Eddy once said in her classroom, "There is a vast difference between the meaning of the words 'human' and 'mortal.' When you become human you are approaching the divine. Jesus was divinely human." It is recorded in Science and Health of Jesus, "Through the magnitude of his human life, he demonstrated the divine Life." (p. 54).

If the dual nature of Jesus is seemingly difficult to clarify, he removed any mysticism about it in his conversation with the Samaritan woman at the well. She had already accepted the prophetic Scripture about the promised Messiah, "which is called Christ," but "Jesus saith unto her, I that speak unto thee am he." (John 4:26). He did not speak of himself as a type, symbol, or illustration of that prophecy. He insisted that the one who was talking with her was the promised Messiah. Because he fulfilled the prophecy, he was greater than the prophecy. Again, he said to the man born blind, "Dost thou believe on the Son of God? He answered and said, Who is he, Lord, that I might believe on him? And Jesus said unto him, Thou hast both seen him, and it is he that talketh with thee." (John 9:35-37). Peter saw the coincidence of the human and the divine in his Master when he declared, "Thou art the Christ, the Son of the living God." Then Jesus was quick to answer, "Blessed art thou, Simon Barjona: for flesh and blood hath not revealed it unto thee, but my Father which is in heaven." (Matt. 16:16, 17). Thus

Peter was justly commended for acknowledging that divinity reaches humanity through the incarnation of Truth.

God had outlined a prophetic figure who could be seen and heard humanly. But the natural man refused to believe that Jesus was the Son of God. It was the natural man who said, "Is not this Jesus, the son of Joseph, whose father and mother we know? how is it then that he saith, I came down from heaven?" (John 6:42). The Apostle Paul said, "The natural man receiveth not the things of the Spirit of God: for they are foolishness unto him: neither can he know them, because they are spiritually discerned." (I Cor. 2:14). Concerning the doubts of the natural man, Mrs. Eddy says, "There is to-day danger of repeating the offence of the Jews by limiting the Holy One of Israel and asking: 'Can God furnish a table in the wilderness?' What cannot God do?" (Science and Health, p. 135).

One of the most important utterances which Jesus ever made is expressed in a parable about the kingdom of heaven. He said, "The kingdom of heaven is like unto leaven, which a woman took, and hid in three measures of meal, till the whole was leavened;" and he added that this woman had "been kept secret from the foundation of the world." (Matt. 13:33, 35). If we accept that prophecy as true, we have an added proof of how God can and does outline. In fact, God outlined just how this woman of prophecy must place in Science, Theology, and Medicine the leaven of the Comforter, until the whole of mortal thought would be changed "as yeast changes the chemical properties of meal." (Science and Health, p. 118).

The divine Message, humanly expressed, has always come through a divinely sent Messenger. The advent of the Messenger always precedes the Message. Moses, the Messenger, preceded the revelation of the Ten Commandments. Being a revelation, the Ten Commandments are based on nothing written, and they are inseparable from the Hebrew Lawgiver. In like manner, the promised Messiah came first as the incarnate Jesus, and then followed Christ's Christianity. Christ Jesus is indeed inseparable from his message of Christianity. He prophesied the coming of the Comforter which should be the final Revelation, together with the Woman "kept secret from the foundation of the world." Mrs. Eddy declares that this Comforter is Divine Science, — her only ideal, and that "the individual and his ideal can never be severed. If either is misunderstood or maligned, it eclipses the other with the shadow cast by this error." (Miscellaneous Writings, p. 105). Divine Science is indeed "the second appearing in the flesh of the Christ," as Science and Health declares (p. 118).

It is true that Deity is never outlined, but it is equally certain that Deity outlined His own creation to Moses, and that outline is recorded in the first chapter of Genesis in the Bible. Humanity had received a direct communication from God that was fully outlined. The record begins with the creative mandate, "Let there be light: and there was light." (Gen.1:3). But the Children of Israel saw in that light an unsolved mystery. Here was a light that preceded the sun, and had nothing to do with solar light; yet it was a light that revealed spiritual creation, and Moses was the divinely selected Messenger to record it.

With that revelation concerning the light, Moses gained a distinct impression which he recorded in these words: "The Lord thy God will raise up unto thee a Prophet from the midst of thee, of thy brethren, like unto me; unto him ye shall hearken." (Deut. 18:15). Here was a promised Messiah or God-sent Messenger by whom divinity could reach humanity, however obscure that light might seem to be.

In the course of time, other spiritual seers began to interpret that light, until Isaiah saw in prophetic vision that "The people that walked in darkness have seen a great light: . . . For unto us a child is born, unto us a son is given: and the government shall be upon his shoulder: . . . Of the increase of his government and peace there shall be no end . . . The zeal of the Lord of hosts will perform this." (Isa. 9:2, 6, 7).

As spiritually-minded men became better acquainted

with their heavenly Father, they enlarged their concept of the light that must be personified as a promised Messiah. As the time approached for that prophecy to be fulfilled, it became an accepted teaching of Holy Writ that this promised Messiah would be born in the little town of Bethlehem, and that he would be a ruler in Israel.

The law by which divinity reaches humanity was not revealed to the Hebrews until they were made ready for it. For forty years they were schooled in self-discipline so as to do by nature the things contained in the law. Then they received the Ten Commandments which have survived human lawlessness. In like manner the Children of Israel were being prepared to understand the light in spiritual creation as the incarnation of Truth, by which divinity reaches humanity.

Webster defines "incarnate" as that which is invested with bodily nature or human form; hence personified. The chosen people were being prepared to accept the incarnation of that light which God revealed to Moses. Thus John the Baptist was sent from God to bear witness of that Light. John declared "He was not that Light, but was sent to bear witness of that Light." Being a spiritual seer, John recognized Jesus as the personification of that Light, and he said, "Behold the Lamb of God, which taketh away the sin of the world." (John 1:29). Mrs. Eddy writes, "Such Christians as John cognize the symbols of God, reach the sure foundations of time, stand upon the shore of eternity, and grasp and gather — in all glory — what eye hath not seen." (Miscellaneous Writings, p. 82). And so it was that Jesus confessed and said, "I am the light of the world: he that followeth me shall not walk in darkness, but shall have the light of life." (John 8:12).

There has been a great deal of mysticism built around that light which was made to appear on the first day of creation. But Jesus clarified it in his discourse on the Door of the sheepfold. His disciples did not understand his parable at first, so he explained it by declaring, "I am the door of the sheep," and "No man cometh unto the Father, but by me." (John 10:7, 14:6).

Suppose, for example, that we have a furnished room in utter darkness. As we turn on the light, those furnishings are made to appear, to become visible. They were not created by the light; they were already present. It is the office of the light to make those furnishings, already created, visible to all. So it is the office of the Christ-light to make the creations of our heavenly Father visible to all, through the Door of the sheepfold. Then creation could look back through that same Door and behold our heavenly Father. Thus it has become an accepted teaching of theology that divinity reaches humanity through Christ's coming.

This Door is a recognized form of government when we remember Jesus' continued explanation, "If any man enter in, he shall be saved." (John 10:9). Then he sounded the warning that if any man seeks to climb up some other way, he is likened to a thief and a robber; to one who would steal, kill, or destroy; but he who enters the heavenly kingdom by the Door, is granted life in abundance. It is like one who gains membership in the Christian Science Church in strict conformity to the provisions of the Church Manual. If the Manual requirements are craftily circumvented, and one climbs up some other way, he is classified by the Master Christian as a thief and a robber, who kills and destroys. To maintain the unity and purity of the Church, all must enter by the Door which God revealed to the author of that Church Manual, for it relates to the problem of salvation.

When Jesus likened his office of Christ to the Door of the heavenly kingdom, he explained a secondary office which he held, which he likened to the Shepherd of the sheep. It was the prophet Ezekiel who said, "And ye my flock, the flock of my pasture, are men, and I am your God, saith the Lord God." (Ezek. 34:31). The good Shepherd is, therefore, the leader of his flock, who watches over them and protects them from being scattered by wolves in sheep's clothing. Thus Christ Jesus qualifies in a secondary office, in another form of government, as the Shepherd of the sheep.

More light is thrown on this secondary office when Jesus prophesies the coming of another Comforter, which he defines as "the Spirit of truth," which "will guide you into all truth." (John 16:13). His reference to "another Comforter" implies that he was one Comforter, and that there must be another, making them complementary to each other. The only reference to two such lights in the heavenly kingdom is on the fourth day of spiritual creation. Those lights as incarnations of Truth were created to be rulers in Israel, another distinctive form of government.

It required about fifteen hundred years for God's people to learn about the incarnation of Truth in its application to the light of the first day of creation; and it required another two thousand years for God's people to apply that same teaching to the two great lights of the fourth day. Mrs. Eddy writes in Science and Health (p. 501), "The incarnation of Truth, . . . God illustrated by light and harmony." That is an outline of God's method for reaching the needs of humanity, exemplified in God's two witnesses, Christ Jesus and Mary Baker Eddy.

In the writing of Science and Health, Mrs. Eddy discovered "a strange coincidence or relationship with the light of revelation and solar light." (Miscellany, p. 114). She could not write her manuscript "after sunset." Not until the rising of the sun would "the influx of divine interpretation" pour into her spiritual sense. She knew that the divine power, infinitely above herself, dictated Science and Health with Key to the Scriptures. She goes on to say, "I should blush to write of 'Science and Health with Key to the Scriptures' as I have, were it of human origin, and were I, apart from God, its author." Christian Science, like the Ten Commandments, is a revelation that is based on nothing written. Mrs. Eddy has said, "I do not find my authority for Christian Science in history, but in revelation." (Miscellany, p. 318). Christian Science is the second coming of Christ. All revelation must be in agreement, because it has a common origin. The Apostle James writes, "Every good gift and every perfect gift is from above, and cometh down from the Father of lights." (James 1:17).

Let us now consider the two forms of government which God outlined for humanity in the light of the first day of creation, and in the two great lights of the fourth day. The first is clearly stated in the definition of Christ given in our textbook: "The divine manifestation of God, which comes to the flesh to destroy incarnate error." (Science and Health, p. 583). Mrs. Eddy also refers to "the incarnate Jesus" as "that life-link forming the connection through which the real reaches the unreal, Soul rebukes sense, and Truth destroys error." (Science and

Health, p. 350). This explains Jesus' reference to himself as the Door. It also indicates that divinity reaches humanity equally through Messenger and Message.

In defending his Messianic claims, Jesus said, "I have greater witness than that of John: for the works which the Father hath given me to finish, the same works that I do, bear witness of me, that the Father hath sent me." (John 5:36). Then he summarized those works as follows: "the blind see, the lame walk, the lepers are cleansed, the deaf hear, the dead are raised, to the poor the gospel is preached. And blessed is he, whosoever shall not be offended in me." (Luke 7:22, 23). This describes the form of government implied in Christ's coming. It is the Truth that makes one free in mind and body.

And how can a true Christian make this Truth practical? Mrs. Eddy writes, "The rays of infinite Truth, when gathered into the focus of ideas, bring light instantaneously." (Science and Health, p. 504). This statement describes Christ's coming. To bring an idea into focus is to clarify it. If a light is thrown upon a screen, the lenses are adjusted to bring that light into pencilled clarity. In like manner, the student must bring those scattered rays of spiritual Truth into the focus and clarity of ideas. One must be a doer of the Word, and not just a hearer of the Word. The student must bring himself into obedience to that which is true in the sight of God. Those who are healed by the reading of Science and Health have yielded their allegiance to the system or form of government exemplified in Christ's coming. The student is emancipated from human bondage by that light of Truth which is above the sun.

Now let us examine the "light" in the first chapter of Genesis which is mentioned on the fourth day of spiritual creation. There is no longer one light, but two great lights. They are created to be rulers in the heavenly kingdom, — another reference to government. Here is where the natural man takes violent issue with the incarnation of Truth. He may go along peaceably with the incarnation of the one great light on the first day of creation as the Christ light; but when he comes to the incarnation of the two great lights on the fourth day, his human resistance takes over.

Webster informs us that a ruler is one who exercises the governing power commonly associated with a king; it is to have the power of command, the power of supreme authority. It is a collective form of government, with the power to make laws to govern a collective whole.

This word "rule," mentioned on the fourth day of creation, is from a Hebrew primitive root (mashal), meaning to rule or have dominion. It combines governor with reign, having power. Then we come to something very interesting: from another Hebrew word (menshalah), which is the feminine of "minshal," there is another type of ruler, or power to rule. The lesson to be gained from the analysis of those two Hebrew words is that the two great lights introduce the masculine and feminine aspects of rulership. Mrs. Eddy makes it clear that, prior to the fourth day of creation, "The feminine gender is not yet expressed in the text." (Science and Health, p. 508).

We are indebted to the prophet Micah for calling attention to the two great rulers in the heavenly kingdom, and that one is a man and the other is a woman. As for the man, he must be born in Bethlehem, of Judea, which points to Christ Jesus. The woman is the woman in travail, who must bring forth "a man child" who is "caught up unto God, and to his throne." (Rev. 12:5). This ruler, God's idea, "will eventually rule all nations and peoples — imperatively, absolutely, finally — with divine Science." (Science and Health, p. 565).

Micah's prophecy (Micah 5:2, 3) identifies those two rulers in the heavenly kingdom as having been "from of old, from everlasting," which places them in the first chapter of Genesis. "The incarnation of Truth . . . which God illustrated by light and harmony," of which Science and Health speaks, can now be recognized in the fourth day as a man and a woman. Referring to the star of Bethlehem, which is also the star of Boston, Mrs. Eddy writes, "Led by a solitary star amid the darkness, the Magi of old foretold the Messiahship of Truth. Is the wise man of to-day believed, when he beholds the light which heralds Christ's eternal dawn and describes its effulgence?" (p. 95). Jesus once said, "Whoso readeth, let him understand."

Who is it that doubts this prophecy and labels it mysticism? Let us hear Mrs. Eddy's answer: "Take courage, dear reader, for any seeming mysticism surrounding realism is explained in the Scripture, 'There went up a mist from the earth (matter);' and the mist of materialism will vanish as we approach spirituality, the realm of reality; cleanse our lives in Christ's righteousness; bathe in the baptism of Spirit, and awake in His likeness." (Miscellaneous Writings, p. 30).

Mrs. Eddy refers to John the Baptist as antedating his own existence. "He who knew the foretelling Truth, beheld the forthcoming Truth, as it came up out of the baptism of Spirit, to enlighten and redeem mortals." (Miscellaneous Writings, p. 82). There is indeed a pre-existence, as Christian Science teaches, and Jesus is the only one who remembered his own preexistence well enough to have it placed on record. He also understood and recorded the preexistence of the Woman with the leaven, together with her message, the promised Comforter, which we recognize in divine Science. But the Adam Dream has no antecedent.

There is no contradiction in the teaching that the Adam

Dream has no antecedent, even if one assumes that a mortal, or anything human, must be wholly erroneous. The natural man may go so far as to claim that the human identity of Jesus and of Mrs. Eddy were unknown to God, but only the natural man or dreamer would fall into such a trap. We have a Bible Lesson entitled "Mortals and Immortals," given us for study twice each year. That Bible Lesson develops the fact that to the degree that a mortal achieves the ability to overcome sin, disease, and death, he gains immortality. This poses the question, Can there be any good in the human consciousness? Mrs. Eddy replies, "The more I understand true humanhood, the more I see it to be sinless, — as ignorant of sin as is the perfect Maker." (Unity of Good, p. 49). This indicates a progressive state out of mortality into immortality. It leads to her explanation of the transparency of goodness, whether expressed humanly or otherwise. (Science and Health, p. 295).

Looking deeper into the mortal dream, we learn that it has no reality nor intelligence, and that "Mortals are the Adam dreamers." (Science and Health, p. 249). But we learn also that one may become aware in his dream that it is a dream. With the coming of that awareness, the dreamer awakens. Even if one's mind awakens sooner than his body, the awareness of a fact ends the dream. Mrs. Eddy says, "The mortal mind through which Truth appears most vividly is that one which has lost much materiality — much error — in order to become a better transparency for Truth." (Science and Health, p. 295). One would continue to dwell in dreamland but for Truth's awakening. "The great verities of existence are never excluded by falsity," says Mrs. Eddy (Science and Health, p. 543), otherwise we would lose our concept of an omnipresent God. This was made clear when the Angel Gabriel was sent from God to the Virgin Mary, to her correct domicile, and revealed to her the verities of spiritual creation in the Fatherhood of God, leaving with her the assurance that "with God nothing shall be impossible." (Luke 1:37).

Mary was informed by this same Angel Gabriel that she would bring forth a son who would be ruler in Israel, "and of his kingdom there shall be no end." (Luke 1:33). As a ruler in Israel, this same Christ Jesus was able to prove that he could enter a closed room, when the door was locked. As the immaculate idea of God, he could also enter a closed consciousness and break down the middle wall of partition that would separate a mortal from an immortal, and enable one's prayers to reach the human need. And why? Because Christ is "The divine manifestation of God, which comes to the flesh to destroy incarnate error." (Science and Health, p. 583). This same Christ could awaken "Lazarus from the dream" of death and "improve on a false sense." (Science and Health, p. 493). Thus it is that divinity can and does reach humanity through the governing power of Christ and so proves that "In the desolation of human understanding, divine Love hears and answers the human call for help." (Miscellaneous Writings, p. 81).

The first chapter of Genesis and the Holy City have much in common. This City of our God is a "holy habitation" which has neither boundary nor limits. Instead of walled sides, which imply an enclosure with limits, Mrs. Eddy has described the Holy City as having four cardinal points. The first of these is the divine Word, "the polar magnet of Revelation," pointing to the North Star. The second cardinal point is Christ, the spiritual idea of God, to which the Wisemen were led by the star of Bethlehem. The works which Jesus performed as the Good Shepherd, calling his own sheep by name, established Christianity as the third cardinal point in the Holy City. After that comes the promised Comforter, designated as the fourth cardinal point, because it "forever interprets this great example and the great Exemplar." (Science and Health, p. 577).

It was Abraham who first "looked for a city which hath foundations, whose builder and maker is God." (Heb. 11:10). Its four cardinal points became known to Ezekiel as having twelve gates, on which were written the names of the twelve tribes of Israel. The twelve foundations of the City had written on them the names of the twelve apostles of the Lamb. Thus Jesus has been definitely identified with the foundations of the Holy City, "For other foundation can no man lay than that is laid, which is Jesus Christ." (I Cor. 3:11).

This puts at naught the claim made by the Apostle Peter when he declared that "God is no respecter of persons." In his appeal to reason, the Apostle Paul declared that Christ Jesus "was counted worthy of more glory than Moses, inasmuch as he who hath builded the house hath more honour than the house." (Heb. 3:3). So Paul, speaking of Jesus, quotes the Psalmist as saying, "Therefore God, even thy God, hath anointed thee with the oil of gladness above thy fellows." (Heb. 1:9). Consequently, Peter modified his sweeping statement about no respect of persons by adding that Christ Jesus "is Lord of all." (Acts 10:36). Speaking of God's Messenger, Mrs. Eddy says, "What Deity *foreknows*, Deity must *foreordain*; else He is not omnipotent." (Unity of Good, p. 19).

That Christ Jesus was foreordained is indicated in his report as a masterbuilder. He said, "Be of good cheer; I have overcome the world." Then addressing himself to God, he said, "I have finished the work which thou gavest me to do." Howbeit, he explained to the people, "I have yet many things to say unto you, but ye cannot bear them

now." To clarify his meaning about this unfinished business, he told about the promised Comforter, who must
bring the final revelation, leading into all Truth.

God outlined this promised Comforter to Jesus, who
was fully informed about that assignment, but Jesus was
not permitted to carry it out. His work was finished, and
the new assignment was left for the Woman to do. God
outlined or described that Woman to Jesus, and Jesus in
turn repeated that pattern of the Woman to John on Patmos. She was foreknown by Deity, and foreordained,
because her work or assignment was complementary to
that of Christ Jesus.

The "woman in travail," mentioned by Micah as a ruler
in Israel, "is crowned with twelve stars." Mrs. Eddy
identifies this group of twelve as "The twelve tribes of
Israel with all mortals." Then she goes on to say, "These
are the stars in the crown of rejoicing." (Science and
Health, p. 562). The "woman in travail," the woman
God-crowned, was not self-appointed by any act of her
own, to carry out her assignment. Her assignment was
what God revealed to Christ Jesus in the opening verse of
the book of Revelation. Then God amplified His revelation to Christ Jesus by describing the woman "kept secret
from the foundation of the world." God also outlined her
assignment, which Jesus then dictated to John on Patmos.
Her assignment included the writing of Science and

Health, and of our Church Manual. In the course of time, God actually *dictated* those two books to Mary Baker Eddy. She was the chosen vessel. She writes, "God had been graciously preparing me during many years for the reception of this final revelation of the absolute divine Principle of scientific mental healing." (Science and Health, p. 107).

We might ask, What is meant by the saying "during many years?" To the natural man it might mean a period of time beginning with the year 1866, when Mrs. Eddy had her healing. To the spiritually-minded one, those "many years" could take us back to the fourth day of creation, to the two great lights who were created to rule over the heavenly kingdom, — the male and female of God's appointing.

Jesus admitted to Pilate that he had a kingdom, but not of this world. It was a heavenly kingdom. He did not achieve that kingdom by conquest, by self-seeking, nor did he try to prepare himself for any such eventuality, as the natural man might believe. Jesus told Pilate, "To this end was I born, and for this cause came I into the world, that I should bear witness unto the truth." (John 18:37). God prepared him, even as God prepared Mary Baker Eddy, to be a ruler in Israel. Being a God-ordained ruler, Jesus made a new commandment, "That ye love one another, as I have loved you." (John 15:12). In like manner, Mary

Baker Eddy has given us a form of government in our Church Manual, for she was invested with deific power to make laws as a ruler in the heavenly kingdom. So the destiny of The Mother Church has its place in the Holy City, and membership in this Church becomes a factor in achieving one's citizenship in the New Jerusalem.

Then let us consider the membership of that Church, namely the hundred and forty-four thousand who are the redeemed of the Lord. That redemption requires self-discipline, and Christian Science is the greatest disciplinarian humanly known. It introduces a third form of government, established by the creative Mind, and fully described in the first chapter of Genesis. This is the inherent right of dominion which God gave to the sons and daughters of God. The man who appeared on the sixth day of creation was given dominion over the fish of the sea, over the fowl of the air, and over the cattle and creeping things of the earth. This government is an individual power over lesser ideas, including that of self-government. Man is not granted power, however, over his brothers and sisters. That collective power of government is vested only in the two anointed ones who were created to be rulers in Israel.

The word "dominion" comes from a primitive root in the Hebrew tongue, namely, "radah." It means to "tread down or subjugate; to prevail against." This is a type of individual or self-government, by which one works out his own salvation; that is, salvation from sin, disease, and death. Describing spiritual man Mrs. Eddy says, "His birthright is dominion, not subjection." (Science and Health, p. 518).

Any seeming complexity in these three forms of government in the first chapter of Genesis may be clarified by the following simplified statement in Science and Health (p. 503): "Immortal and divine Mind presents the idea of God: *first,* in light; *second,* in reflection; *third,* in spiritual and immortal forms of beauty and goodness." This statement does not describe three ideas, nor even two ideas. It presents three footsteps in the spiritual unfoldment of the one idea of God, — the spiritual unfoldment of that Light which is above the sun. The first step is the appearing of the Christ-light as a subjective idea in the God-head, with which Jesus is identified. The second step is the reflection of that same idea in what we know as generic man, identified with the Woman in the Apocalypse. The third step presents the same idea as "spiritual and immortal forms of beauty and goodness," in other words, the sons and daughters of God. These are the hundred and forty-four thousand who are the redeemed of the Lord.

When God called Moses to lead the Hebrews out of Egyptian bondage, He appeared in a flame of fire in a bush, and the bush was not consumed. When Moses proved that he had enough spirituality to respond to that incarnation of Truth, the voice of God spoke to him out of the bush. "The Soul-inspired patriarchs," as we read in Science and Health (p. 308), "heard the voice of Truth, and talked with God as consciously as man talks with man." As the Children of Israel took up their journey through the Red Sea and the Wilderness, "the Lord went before them by day in a pillar of a cloud, to lead them the way; and by night in a pillar of fire, to give them light; to go by day and night." (Ex. 13:21). And when they came to Mt. Sinai, "the Lord descended upon it in fire," and spoke with the voice of a trumpet, uttering the law of the Ten Commandments, by which divinity reaches humanity.

Again, when God required Moses to record the Ten Commandments on two tables of stone, the whole mountain burned with fire; and as Moses came down from the Mount, the skin of his face shone, so that the Children of Israel were afraid to come near him. Then Moses placed a vail over his face, while speaking to the Children of Israel; but he took off the vail when he spoke to God. That was the vail of matter which still beclouds the reading of the Old Testament, or until Christian Science has come with the clear explanation of the incarnation of Truth.

When Israel was halting between two opinions, Elijah

challenged the prophets of Baal with an answer by fire. Baal gave no answer; but when Elijah called upon the God of Israel, fire came down and consumed the burnt offerings, and even licked up the water in the trenches. Then the people gladly turned to the worship of the God of Israel. As the time approached for Elijah to be translated, "there appeared a chariot of fire, and horses of fire, . . . and Elijah went up by a whirlwind into heaven." (II Kings 2:11).

On the Mount of Transfiguration, the face of Jesus "did shine as the sun, and his raiment was white as the light." A bright cloud overshadowed them, and "a voice out of the cloud" said, "This is my beloved Son, in whom I am well pleased; hear ye him." Moses and Elijah were talking with Jesus on the Mount, not about his decease, but about his departure from Jerusalem. This was Jesus' first overcoming of death for himself, as the following use of the word "again" would indicate, when he cautioned his disciples to "Tell the vision to no man, until the Son of man be risen again from the dead." (Matt. 17:9). After conquering death the second time, Jesus instructed his disciples to remain in Jerusalem until the Holy Ghost should come upon them, as it did on the Pentecostal Day.

After the family of Noah had survived the Flood, the people thought that they could outwit God, in the event of a second Flood, by building the Tower of Babel. The result was a confusion of tongues. No longer united, a multiplicity of tongues or languages appeared. But on the Day of Pentecost, which marked the celebration of the coming of the Holy Spirit, there was a mighty rushing wind from heaven, followed by tongues of fire which parted and rested upon each of those who were present. It was a baptism of the Holy Ghost, because "they were all filled with the Holy Ghost, and began to speak with other tongues, as the Spirit gave them utterance," (Acts 2:4), for every man heard in his own language. The people were once again united in their Mother-tongue, under their Father-Mother God. Deity, which is never outlined, had outlined this remarkable experience.

The incarnation of Truth was again manifested when Saul was made a convert to Christianity on his way to Damascus. At midday, a light above the sun overshadowed him, and a voice said, "Saul, Saul, why persecutest thou me?" When Saul asked, "Who art thou, Lord?" the voice said, "I am Jesus whom thou persecutest: it is hard for thee to kick against the pricks." (Acts 9:1-9). A fact is established by the testimony of two witnesses, the other witness in this case being Ananias, who was directed by the same voice to go to the street address of Saul and heal him. It is believed that the conversion of Saul occurred two or three years after the crucifixion and ascension of Jesus.

In later years, this same Apostle Paul wrote: "I knew a man in Christ above fourteen years ago, (whether in the body, I cannot tell; or whether out of the body, I cannot tell: God knoweth;) . . . and heard unspeakable words, which it is not lawful for a man to utter. Of such an one will I glory." (II Cor. 12:2-5). This is another illustration of how Deity reached humanity through the incarnation of Truth.

Nor is this all. We have a prophecy concerning the latter days which remains to be fulfilled. Jesus told his disciples "that all things must be fulfilled, which were written in the law of Moses, and in the prophets, and in the psalms, concerning me." (Luke 24:44). The doom of Gog and Magog, first recorded by the prophet Ezekiel, and repeated by Christ Jesus in the book of Revelation, is still in its formative experience.

In her message to First Church of Christ, Scientist, London, England, Mrs. Eddy writes: "Satan is unchained only for a season, as the Revelator foresaw." (Miscellany, p. 201). And why must Satan be set loose? So that Gog and Magog may follow their destiny and deceive the nations in the four quarters of the earth, and bring them together in battle: "the number of whom is as the sand of the sea." (Rev. 20:8). In other words, the problem of these latter days is how to cope with deception. It is a repetition of the problem which Elijah encountered when the people were of two opinions concerning the true God. To-day, it is the great Red Dragon who wages war on the Woman God-crowned. "This dragon stands for the sum total of human error," as Mary Baker Eddy declares. (Science and Health, p. 563). This dragon seeks to break the Ten Commandments, by which divinity reaches humanity, and to deceive the whole world.

The Revelator makes it clear that this dragon continues its warfare on the Woman's seed, who keep the Commandments of God. It is the dragon who fosters the deep-seated opposition to any personification of the two great lights which appeared on the fourth day of creation. And why? Because that line of attack would obscure the method of God's appearing to humanity.

Any obscuration of how divinity reaches humanity is a basic form of deception. It is so deceptive that one might ask, what does it profit me or benefit me to know about the incarnation of Truth? The answer is contained in the account of the baptism of the eunuch by the Apostle Philip. (Acts 8:37).

The question was once put to Mrs. Eddy, "Did the salvation of the eunuch depend merely on his believing that Jesus Christ was the Son of God?" (Miscellaneous Writings, p. 77). She replied emphatically, "It did." Then she went on to say: "Philip's requirement was, that he should not only acknowledge the incarnation, — God made manifest through man, — but even the eternal unity of man and God." That acknowledgment of the incarnation, by which Christ Jesus could be recognized as the Son of God, meant "to enter unshod the Holy of Holies, where the miracle of grace appears, and where the miracles of Jesus had their birth." From this we conclude that the problem of salvation from sin, disease, and death can be solved only to the degree that we understand the incarnation of Truth, by which divinity reaches humanity through God's own anointed Messengers, together with their Messages, as revealed in Christian Science.

Since Mary Baker Eddy has established the fact that "the incarnate Jesus" is indeed "that life-link forming the connection through which the real reaches the unreal, Soul rebukes sense, and Truth destroys error," (Science and Health, p. 350), we learn that divinity reaches humanity through God's Messenger as definitely as through His Message. In fact, Mrs. Eddy says of her own ministry, "Christian Science is my only ideal; and the individual and his ideal can never be severed. If either is misunderstood or maligned, it eclipses the other with the shadow cast by this error." (Miscellaneous Writings, p. 105).

The Dragon, in its purpose to deceive "the nations in the four quarters of the earth," makes war on the Woman and on those of her seed who keep the Commandments of God. It is the Dragon which opposes the incarnation of the two great lights on the fourth day of spiritual creation. That is "the obstacle which the serpent, sin, would impose between man and his creator." (Science and Health, p. 338). The attack is, therefore, against both Messenger and Message which Deity has outlined for reaching the needs of humanity. But Science and Health gives us the blessed assurance that "In this age the earth will help the woman; the spiritual idea will be understood." (p. 570).

XIV

PROPHECY

"THE MOTHER CHURCH."
"THE FIRST CHURCH OF CHRIST SCIENTIST."

Mary Baker G. Eddy and James F. Gilman, Artists*
*Original Caption

---*---

Prophecy

PROPHECY involves the genius of faith. Some people underestimate the element of faith, and some discount it entirely; whereas faith is the open door to every department of learning. When for example, the child goes to school, he must at first accept on faith his teacher's declaration that two and two make four. He must accept on faith the declaration of his teacher about the letters of the alphabet. Think of the tremendous faith the inventors of the telegraph, the telephone, and the wireless systems must have had. Think of the magnificent faith of our aviators, who have ventured to all parts of the globe in their mastery of the air. Then we begin to realize that the open door to every department of learning, discovery, and invention is faith. In fact, no one can achieve anything really worth while except through faith.

Mrs. Eddy has written in her book, Science and Health (p. 298), that spiritual realities "dawn in faith and glow full-orbed in spiritual understanding." Consequently, faith is that element of intelligence where divinity reaches humanity. The book of Hebrews declares that "faith is the substance of things hoped for, the evidence of things not seen."

When God required Moses to lead the Hebrew people out of Egypt, they had to have faith before they could accept him as their God-appointed leader. If they were lacking in faith, they would have to remain in Egyptian darkness. But God knew how to convince the people, and He gave to Moses two signs or symbols which would be acceptable to the people of faith. The first was the use of the rod, which when it was cast down, became a serpent. The second was the healing of Moses' hand of leprosy. Then God assured Moses that if the Hebrews would not believe the first sign of the rod, they would believe the latter sign of healing. And so the sign of healing did convince the people that Moses was their God-appointed leader.

When John the Baptist sent messengers to inquire if Jesus were the promised Messiah, Jesus showed the same sign of healing which God Himself had given to Moses fifteen hundred years before. Turning to the bystanders, Jesus proceeded in that same hour to heal many of their plagues and infirmities. Then he replied to the messengers, "Go your way, and tell John what things ye have seen and heard; how that the blind see, the lame walk, the lepers are cleansed, the deaf hear, the dead are raised, to the poor the gospel is preached" (Luke 7:22). Those cases of healing indicated exactly what Jesus meant by "works" when he said, "I have greater witness than that of John: for the works which the Father hath given me to finish, the same works that I do, bear witness of me, that the Father hath sent me" (John 5:36). For, "though ye believe not me, believe the works" (*ibid.*, 10:38).

John the Baptist had the necessary faith to accept the works of healing as sufficient proof that Jesus was the promised Messiah. But three days after the crucifixion of Christ Jesus, two of his followers were discussing those momentous happenings while traveling to Emmaus; and "Jesus himself drew near, and went with them." Evidently the experiences of the crucifixion and the resurrection had greatly changed his personal appearance, because his students did not recognize him; and his questions made them think that he must be a stranger in those parts. From their expressions of grief and sadness, Jesus learned that their faith in his works of healing was not sufficient to convince them that he was indeed the promised Messiah, as it had John the Baptist, because they were believing that his ministry had failed. What then, could be done to rescue his great work from total eclipse? Jesus first rebuked them for their unbelief, or lack of faith. Then, "beginning at Moses and all the prophets, he expounded unto them in all the scriptures the things concerning himself" (Luke 24:27).

Just why was this Scriptural exegesis so necessary? Jesus had already explained the reason in his account of the rich man and Lazarus. When the rich man appealed to Abraham to warn his father's house of his torments, on the assumption that they would listen to one who had risen from the dead, Abraham replied, "If they hear not Moses and the prophets, neither will they be persuaded, though one rose from the dead" (Luke 16:31).

This account is most revealing; it is an astonishing admission. Jesus foresaw that a simple faith in his ministry would not maintain the loyalty of his followers. He foresaw that his mighty works of healing, and even his raising of the dead, would be insufficient to guarantee their loyalty to his Messiahship unless that loyalty was based on prophetic vision. What seemed to be a lost cause could be rescued only to the degree that his followers were willing to see and acknowledge his place in Scriptural prophecy, in God's plan of salvation. Above all, they must realize that his ministry stemmed directly from God, and must therefore have a place in creation as recorded in the first chapter of Genesis.

After the walk to Emmaus, Jesus discovered that his own disciples had indeed lost their faith in his mission. When he suddenly appeared in their midst, "they were terrified and affrighted, and supposed that they had seen a spirit." But he reassured them by saying, "a spirit hath not flesh and bones, as ye see me have." Then he took a piece of broiled fish and some honeycomb and ate before them, so that they were convinced that he had indeed risen from the dead. "And he said unto them, These are the words which I spake unto you, while I was yet with you, that all things must be fulfilled, which were written in the law of Moses, and in the prophets, and in the psalms, concerning me. Then opened he their understanding, that they might understand the scriptures" (Luke 24:44–45). So an understanding of the Scriptures is conditional upon one's ability to see, through faith, what is recorded in Bible prophecy, "For Moses truly said unto the fathers, A prophet shall the Lord your God raise up unto you of your brethren, like unto me; him shall ye hear in all things whatsoever he shall say unto you" (Acts 3:22).

It may be that their daily association with Jesus made it difficult for the disciples to believe that the son of a carpenter could have a place in Bible prophecy. Such a human estimate of him exposed them to the temptations of desertion and disloyalty. Now we find Jesus providing the remedy by showing his disciples his place in prophecy, in God's plan of salvation. Such a comprehensive view gave a new meaning to the visible idea, and the disciples were never again tempted with disloyalty.

Before Christ Jesus finished his ministry, he promised to send us another Comforter. That word "another" is significant. It indicates that Christ Jesus himself was one Comforter, and that his method of bringing comfort to the sick and sorrowing was through his works of healing. Then he promised another Comforter, which he described as the "Spirit of truth," which "will guide you into all truth." From that time Christians have been looking for the coming of this promised Comforter, just as the Jews had hitherto been looking for the coming of the promised Messiah. Then what would be the sign of its coming? Would it not be the historic sign of healing? When the people of faith recognize the mighty healing works of Christian Science today, they ask, Is not this the "Spirit of truth," the promised Comforter? The answer is the same that Jesus gave, the "works that I do, bear witness of me, that the Father hath sent me;" for "though ye believe not me, believe the works."

There may be some Christian Scientists who have seen in Mary Baker Eddy only another religious leader, and it may be difficult for them to believe that Mark Baker's daughter could have a place in Bible prophecy. But that human estimate of her exposes one to the whisperings of desertion and disloyalty, which may explain why, according to Daniel's dates, her title of Leader is the last to be generally acknowledged. However, when we today take the walk to Emmaus, and discover her place in Bible prophecy, the visible idea will have a new meaning for us.

The Scriptures will be opened to us as we gain a comprehensive view of prophecy in its application to both Jesus and to the Woman. If such prophecies place them above their fellows, the Psalmist has already conceded that fact concerning Jesus by declaring that "God hath anointed thee with the oil of gladness above thy fellows" (Ps. 45:7).

Since these two prophetic figures occupy a position that is above their fellows, as the 45th Psalm plainly indicates, then we should be able to find them in the first chapter of Genesis, which is a record of spiritual creation. In this record of spiritual creation, light is used symbolically. Its first appearance comes as the immediate result of the divine command, "Let light be, and light was." Mrs. Eddy gives a metaphysical significance to this light that appeared on the first day of creation. She explains that this light "is not from the sun nor from volcanic flames," but it is the spiritual revelation of divine Truth. David in the Psalms, Isaiah, Daniel, and other prophets have joined with Moses in giving a metaphysical meaning to that light which was the first mandate of creative Mind. In a prophecy of Christ's coming, Isaiah describes Christ's office, and tells how God shall keep him "for a light of the Gentiles; to open their blind eyes" (Isa. 42:1–7).

When the parents of Jesus took the babe to Jerusalem, "to present him to the Lord," there was a devout Jew in the temple, Simeon by name, who had the promise from the Holy Ghost "that he should not see death, before he had seen the Lord's Christ." When Simeon saw the babe, Jesus, brought into the temple, he recognized the fulfill-ment of this promise. Taking the child in his arms, he thanked God that he had seen the Lord's Christ. Re-ferring to Isaiah's prophecy, he said, "Mine eyes have seen thy salvation, which thou hast prepared before the face of all people; a light to lighten the Gentiles, and the glory of thy people Israel" (Luke 2:25–32).

John the Baptist came as a witness to the divine light, and his mission is described in the following words: "There was a man sent from God, whose name was John. The same came for a witness, to bear witness of the Light, that all men through him might believe. He was not that Light, but was sent to bear witness of that Light. That was the true Light, which lighteth every man that cometh into the world" (John 1:6–9). When Jesus came to John for baptism, John recognized that Light as the prom-ised Messiah, and he remarked to two of his disciples, "Behold the Lamb of God." Thus we understand that the light, seen and heralded by the prophets, symbolized the Christ.

The prophet Isaiah saw in spiritual vision what God's Anointed was destined to perform. To prove that Jesus understood the significance of this prophecy, he once went into the synagogue on the Sabbath, and turned to the description which Isaiah gave of Christ's healing ministry. Having read the passage to the congregation, to their amazement "he began to say unto them, This day is this scripture fulfilled in your ears" (Luke 4:21). At another time he said, "I am the light of the world: he that followeth me shall not walk in darkness, but shall have the light of life" (John 8:12). Even his followers in those days were called the "children of light."

It is interesting to note that light appeared on the first day of creation, but two great lights appeared on the fourth day of creation. These are separate acts of the divine will or command, and the two lights on the fourth day, together with the stars, also have a metaphysical meaning. The two great lights are described as "rulers." They introduce the idea of the heavenly kingdom. Mrs. Eddy says that their light is "not a vitalizing property of matter," but spiritual truth "whose seed is in itself" (Science and Health, pp. 510 and 511). She goes on to say that these lights are appointed to rule not over "material darkness and dawn," but over "the successive appearing of God's ideas" (*ibid.*, p. 504). The idea of a heavenly kingdom with promised rulers in Israel must have been what the Jews were awaiting, for both Herod and Pilate feared the advent of a king in Israel.

The stars that appeared on the fourth day of creation

are referred to by Mrs. Eddy when she describes Paul and Jesus in this manner: "Philosophy never has produced, nor can it reproduce, these stars of the first magnitude — fixed stars in the heavens of Soul" (Miscellaneous Writings, p. 360). That Jesus himself should claim to be one of those stars is indicated as follows: "I am the root and the offspring of David, and the bright and morning star" (Rev. 22:16). In this brief verse, Jesus records three important facts. How can he be simultaneously the root and the offspring of David? Here Jesus is referring to his dual nature of the unseen Christ and the visible idea. The third important fact in this statement verifies a precious tradition in Christian history, symbolized by the star of Bethlehem. It marks the dawn of Christianity. "Led by a solitary star amid the darkness," writes Mrs. Eddy, "the Magi of old foretold the Messiahship of Truth. Is the wise man of to-day believed, when he beholds the light which heralds Christ's eternal dawn and describes its effulgence?" (Science and Health, p. 95). The wise men of today follow the "daystar of divine Science, lighting the way to eternal harmony" (*ibid.*, Pref. vii).

When Pilate was examining Jesus, he put the direct question, "Art thou the King of the Jews?" Jesus replied, "My kingdom is not of this world." When Jesus acknowledged having a kingdom, which made him a ruler in Israel, Pilate asked him again, "Art thou a king then?"

Jesus assented, "Thou sayest that I am a king. To this end was I born, and for this cause came I into the world, that I should bear witness unto the truth" (John 18:33, 36, 37). This colloquy gains the admission from Jesus that he had, in addition to the office of Christ, a secondary function or office which was to "bear witness unto the truth."

Herein do we discover the motive of Jesus in teaching students or disciples; it was to establish his kingdom. He said, "If ye continue in my word, then are ye my disciples indeed; And ye shall know the truth, and the truth shall make you free" (John 8:31, 32). His form of government was based on the very nature of truth. Being the essence of freedom, or liberation from bondage, its seed is within itself. It is a spiritual form of government or rulership, with Jesus as its witness, as he acknowledged to Pilate.

Turning to the prophet Micah, we find a prophecy of the Messianic kingdom. He prophesies that out of Bethlehem of Judea "shall he come forth unto me that is to be ruler in Israel; whose goings forth have been from of old, from everlasting" (Micah 5:2). That places the mission of Jesus in creation, and doubtless Jesus made that fact clear to his followers during their walk to Emmaus. He must have explained that the promised ruler in Israel should be born in Bethlehem of Judea, and that his appearing or birth was foretold "from everlasting." This prophecy points unerringly to Jesus, the visible idea. So the "child" was born in Bethlehem, but the "ruler in Israel" was from everlasting.

This Bethlehem babe must continue to rule, according to the prophet Micah, "until the time that she which travaileth hath brought forth" (Micah 5:3). So the second great light that is to be ruler in Israel is described as a "woman in travail." We find a correlative to this in the book of Revelation, where it tells about a "woman in travail" who "brought forth a man child, who was to rule all nations with a rod of iron: and her child was caught up unto God, and to his throne" (Rev. 12:2, 5). So the governing power of this child is under the immediate direction of God.

This is in agreement with Jesus' pronouncement about the Comforter: "Nevertheless I tell you the truth; It is expedient for you that I go away: for if I go not away, the Comforter will not come unto you; but if I depart, I will send him unto you. And when he is come, he will reprove the world of sin, and of righteousness, and of judgment: Of sin, because they believe not on me; Of righteousness, because I go to my Father, and ye see me no more; Of judgment, because the prince of this world is judged" (John 16:7–11). Mrs. Eddy writes, "This Comforter I understand to be Divine Science" (Science and Health,

p. 55). Consequently, both Jesus and Mrs. Eddy understood their prophetic mission, and that they were complementary to each other.

"Science and Health with Key to the Scriptures," by Mary Baker Eddy, contains a complete statement of divine Science. This is "the little book" which Daniel was required to seal "even to the time of the end." Daniel also saw how these two witnesses were the complement of each other. He saw them standing on the banks of a river, "the one on this side of the bank of the river, and the other on that side of the bank of the river" (Dan. 12:5). We learn why he used the symbolism of a river, because Euphrates and Hiddekel, which are rivers of Eden, are defined by Mrs. Eddy as symbolical of divine Science. Above the river of divine Science, Daniel saw a "man clothed in linen." Then one of the two witnesses appealed to this "man clothed in linen" for information about the time when "the little book" would be unsealed. This "man," which we recognize as the Christ, made no appeal, but "sware by him that liveth for ever that it shall be for a time, times, and an half" (Dan. 12:7). "Him that liveth for ever" is God, as is fully explained in the book of Revelation (Rev. 10:6). So we have the relative position of each figure, placed in the same relative position which they occupy in the first chapter of Genesis. Over all is God, who "liveth for ever:" then comes the Christ, who exercises his prerogative that "no man cometh unto the Father, but by" that Christ light, and conveys God's answer to the witness on the riverbank. Then we see the two great lights, or witnesses, whose prerogative is to rule all nations and peoples with divine Science, as Mrs. Eddy states in "the little book." (Science and Health, p. 565). Moreover Daniel said, "The vision of the evening and the morning which was told is true" (Dan. 8:26).

Further light is shed on Daniel's vision by a correlative passage in the book of Revelation which reads, "And he shewed me a pure river of water of life, clear as crystal, proceeding out of the throne of God and of the Lamb" (Rev. 22:1). So the "man" above the river of divine Science in Daniel's vision, is none other than the Lamb, or Christ. Moreover the river of divine Science, in both accounts, emanates from God and the Lamb. That places the Lamb, or Christ, at-one with God, and the remaining seven days of creation, including divine Science and the two witnesses, stem from God and His Christ, or from Principle and its idea. That explains Mrs. Eddy's statement that "Principle and its idea is one" (Science and Health, p. 465), the idea referred to being the Christ.

That divine Science should operate like a river is very significant. If a dam or obstruction is placed in the course of a river, the water backs up and spreads out, until it rises in strength to overpower all obstruction and to overflow the dam. The river of divine Science is likewise irresistible. Its nature is to express life and healing, and its healing of the nations is irresistible.

Zechariah's vision of the two olive trees and of the two candlesticks brings out an added meaning. Instead of a river, Zechariah saw a bowl of "golden oil," supported by a golden candlestick (Zech. 4). This bowl had seven lamps and seven pipes. Seven expresses completeness, and Mrs. Eddy defines "oil" as consecration and heavenly inspiration. So the oil of gladness and consecration, which stems from God, is complete in its illumination and expression. According to "the pattern in the mount," the gold used in this description is a reference to Deity, and the golden lamps and pipes are the divine modes of expressing the spiritual nature of divine Science.

Then we may ask, "What are these two olive trees upon the right side of the candlestick and upon the left side thereof . . . which through the two golden pipes empty the golden oil out of themselves?" The answer is that "These are the two anointed ones, that stand by the Lord of the whole earth" (Zech. 4:11–14).

The correlative in the book of Revelation says, "I will give power unto my two witnesses, and they shall prophesy a thousand two hundred and threescore days, clothed in sackcloth. These are the two olive trees, and the two candlesticks standing before the God of the earth" (Rev.

11:3, 4). The twelve hundred and sixty days is a verifica-
tion of Daniel's date, and Mrs. Eddy accepts it as pointing
to the year 1866, when Christian Science was discovered.

One who gains comfort and inspiration from reading the
Bible must believe the teachings of the prophets. If all
prophecy were deleted from the Bible, there would be little
remaining to inspire hope and faith. Then we might ask,
what would the casual reader gain from the prophetic
utterances about the two witnesses? We know that Jesus
before Pilate declared himself to be one of the two witnesses. Who then might the other witness be? Jesus was
eager to have his followers familiar with his unique position in Bible prophecy. We know too that Mrs. Eddy
was just as eager to have Christian Scientists familiar with
the prophetic utterances about the promised Comforter,
which she specifically identifies as Divine Science. What
Christian Scientists want to know further is whether Mrs.
Eddy can be identified as one of those two witnesses.

In order to satisfy that growing desire, the Christian
Science Board of Directors in April, 1938, appointed a
committee of editors and former editors of the Christian
Science periodicals in order to discover just what Mrs.
Eddy believed concerning herself with respect to Scriptural
prophecy. This committee of six members, trained in
editorial experience, was given access to Mrs. Eddy's
private correspondence, as well as to her published writ-

ings. After prayerfully and carefully studying the evidence, this committee made a report to the Board of Directors of fifty-seven pages of typewritten evidence that Mrs. Eddy regarded herself as having fulfilled Bible prophecy. This extended report was summarized in a brief report which the Directors published in the *Christian Science Sentinel* for June 5, 1943, and also in *The Christian Science Journal* for July, 1943. This report reads as follows:

Mrs. Eddy's Place

The position of The Mother Church as to Mary Baker Eddy's place in the fulfillment of Bible prophecy is clearly set forth in the following paragraphs. These conclusions are not new; they are confirmed by our Leader's writings, and the steadily unfolding fruitage of Christian Science bears witness to their truth.

1. Mrs. Eddy, as the Discoverer and Founder of Christian Science, understood herself to be the one chosen of God to bring the promised Comforter to the world, and, therefore, the revelator of Christ, Truth, in this age.

2. Mrs. Eddy regarded portions of Revelation (that is, Chapter 12) as pointing to her as the one who fulfilled prophecy by giving the full and final revelation of Truth; her work thus being complementary to that of Christ Jesus.

3. As Christ Jesus exemplified the fatherhood of God, she (Mrs. Eddy) revealed God's motherhood; she represents in this age the spiritual idea of God typified by the woman in the Apocalypse. (See Science and Health, 565:13–22.)

4. Mrs. Eddy considered herself to be the "God-appointed" and "God-anointed" messenger to this age, the woman chosen by God to discover the Science of Christian healing and to interpret it to mankind; she is so closely related to Christian Science that a true sense of her is essential to the understanding of Christian Science; in other words, the revelator cannot be separated from the revelation.

5. This recognition of her true status enabled her to withstand the opposition directed against her by "the dragon" (malicious animal magnetism); she was touchingly grateful to those who saw her as the woman of prophecy and who therefore trusted, obeyed, and supported her in her mission.

6. This same recognition is equally vital to our movement, for demonstration is the result of vision; the collecting of this indisputable evidence of our Leader's own view of herself and of her mission marks a great step forward; wisely utilized, this evidence will stimulate and stabilize the growth of Christian Scientists today and in

succeeding generations; it will establish unity in the Field with regard to the vital question of our Leader's relation to Scriptural prophecy.

As we record these important facts, we remind Christian Scientists of our Leader's words (Miscellaneous Writings, p. 308), "The Scriptures and Christian Science reveal 'the way,' and personal revelators will take their proper place in history, but will not be deified."

The Christian Science Board of Directors.

If the fact-finding committee appointed by the Board of Directors has succeeded in satisfying the reader's thought concerning Mrs. Eddy's place in Bible prophecy, then he will be prepared to accept certain conclusions from the opening verse in the book of Revelation. The verse reads as follows: "The Revelation of Jesus Christ, which God gave unto him, to shew unto his servants things which must shortly come to pass; and he sent and signified it by his angel unto his servant John." Many people think of this prophetic book as the revelation of the Apostle John; but the book declares itself to be the revelation of Jesus Christ, and not of John. Being the revelation of Jesus Christ, its vocabulary is that of Jesus, whereas John is but the recorder.

It should be remembered that it was God who gave this revelation to Jesus Christ. God told Jesus of coming events through symbolism. This revelation constituted an act of God. This revelation described ideas of God, ideas as unchanging as God Himself. If one should presume to change or alter in any respect this revelation which God gave to Jesus Christ, such an intent would be comparable to an effort to change creation itself. The authorship of this book has so many important implications that the student should constantly remember its divine origin.

In considering a specific act of creative Mind, we accept the premise that it was God who revealed to Christ Jesus the Woman described in the twelfth chapter of the Apocalypse. Was God in this instance portraying woman in general, or did He describe a specific woman? The text reads "a woman," a specific identity and individuality, not woman in general. This Woman was definitely known to God, and His detailed description of her reveals an identity and individuality as unchanging as God from whom she proceeds. This Woman wears a crown, which identifies her with the heavenly kingdom, signifying that she is a ruler in Israel. This makes her mission an act of God. Moreover, the crown identifies her with the two great lights of the fourth day of creation, since these lights were created to rule.

How is this divine symbolism to be made practical in human experience? The only way by which Moses could convince the people that he was God's appointed messenger was by the sign of the rod and by the healing of leprosy. To convince the people of his time that he too was God's messenger, Jesus was proclaimed by John the Baptist; but Jesus insisted that a greater witness than that of John was his own healing ministry. A third proof of his divine mission was his explanation to his disciples of his place in Bible prophecy. That is to say, the visible idea, Jesus of Nazareth, claimed to be the fulfillment of prophecy. These three steps were required to convince an incredulous people of the divine origin of Jesus.

This same Jesus foretold the coming of the Comforter, which Mrs. Eddy declares is "Divine Science." Moreover, this divine Science as recorded in Science and Health has repeated Jesus' healing ministry. The last chapter in the book entitled "Fruitage," gives evidence that the reading of Science and Health begets the fruitage of Christian healing, which proves its divine origin. But before we could have the divine fruitage of healing, there must appear a messenger or visible idea whom God described to Jesus as a woman in travail. Her child, whom Mrs. Eddy calls divine Science, is also identified with God and His throne.

In her own explanation of Revelation 12:1, Mrs. Eddy makes five distinctive observations concerning the God-crowned woman. Beginning with the marginal heading to the opening paragraph, we read, "True estimate of

God's messenger." In that same paragraph, she speaks about "one whom God has appointed to voice His Word," as the "highest visible idea." So the "highest visible idea," appointed by God "to voice His Word," involves a "true estimate of God's messenger."

Continuing her explanation of Revelation 12:1, we read, "The Revelator saw also the spiritual ideal as a woman clothed in light," etc. But "the light portrayed is really neither solar nor lunar, but spiritual Life, which is 'the light of men'." The third step in this explanation is that "the woman in the Apocalypse symbolizes generic man, the spiritual idea of God." In her concluding paragraph, with the marginal heading "Spiritual idea crowned," she refers to the twelve stars in that crown as "the twelve tribes of Israel with all mortals," which identifies her with the collective idea or generic man. Since the names of the twelve tribes of Israel are in the twelve gates of the Holy City, and the names of the twelve apostles of the Lamb are in the twelve foundations of the Holy City, that makes Jesus ruler over the foundations, and Mrs. Eddy ruler over the gates, by which we enter the Holy City. A further explanation is that this Woman typifies "the spiritual idea of God's motherhood," even as Jesus typified or expressed the fatherhood of God.

In explaining Revelation 12:2, Mrs. Eddy says, "Also the spiritual idea is typified by a woman in travail," etc.

This prophecy fulfills what Micah says about the two rulers in Israel, "whose goings forth have been from of old, from everlasting" (Micah 5:2, 3). "From everlasting" points directly to the two great lights in Genesis, who were created to be rulers in Israel (Gen. 1:16).

Mrs. Eddy says, "The twelfth chapter of the Apocalypse, or Revelation of St. John, has a special suggestiveness in connection with the nineteenth century . . . the distinctive feature has reference to the present age." Thus the visible idea could say, "This prophecy which God gave to Christ Jesus is fulfilled in your ears in the nineteenth century." Only the visible idea could make such a statement.

It was the visible idea who provoked the wrath of the dragon. Is it conceivable that the dragon would be annoyed by a mere type or symbol of womanhood or feminine thought? Science and Health says, "This dragon stands for the sum total of human error" (p. 563). This dragon sought to destroy the child of the visible idea as soon as it was born. When God protected the Woman from the wrath of the dragon by providing a way of escape, then the dragon began to make war upon her seed. The Woman's seed must be those Christian Scientists who keep the Commandments of God and accept the leadership of Mary Baker Eddy, the visible idea.

The Woman whom God described to Christ Jesus was

given a pattern as detailed as the pattern of the tabernacle which God gave to Moses in the mount. The work which this Woman must perform was also given a detailed pattern. This Woman was not selected because of her preparation for the work, any more than Jesus was. The mother of Jesus knew that her unborn babe was the promised Messiah, even before he had any opportunity to prepare himself humanly. These two witnesses were created to rule, and that means they were invested with all the necessary endowments to fulfill their destiny. Far from having been selected at random, this Woman was accurately described two thousand years ago. In fact, it could be said of her, as it was said of Jesus, that her "goings forth have been from of old, from everlasting" (Micah 5:2).

Christian Scientists need to be careful not to deify this visible idea; and they will not, so long as they obey her teachings. She says, "Follow your Leader, only so far as she follows Christ" (1902, Message, p. 4). She also says that her followers will know her best, not through her biographers, but through her writings. When Mrs. Eddy wrote her autobiography, "Retrospection and Introspection," she had to complete the portrayal of herself by quotations from Science and Health. Thus we must become acquainted with the visible idea by reading Science and Health, by understanding her divine modes of thought as God dictated them to her.

That Mary Baker Eddy recognized herself to be the "God-appointed" and "God-anointed" messenger to this age is clearly shown by the following excerpts from her letters. To Ira Knapp she wrote: "I am carrying on a great reform in our ranks through my letters." To Edward A. Kimball, Mrs. Eddy wrote: "For the world to understand me in my true light, and life, would do more for our Cause than all else could. This I learn from the fact that the enemy tries harder to hide these two things from the world than to win any other points. Also Jesus' life and character in their first appearing were treated in like manner."

Mrs. Eddy also wrote to Judge Septimus J. Hanna as follows: "I can do you most good by pointing the path — showing the scenes behind the curtain. The united plan of the evildoers is to cause the beginners either in lecturing or teaching or in our periodicals to keep Mrs. Eddy as she *is* (what God knows of her and revealed to Christ Jesus) out of sight, and to keep her as she *is not* (just another white-haired old lady) constantly before the public. This kills two birds with one stone. It darkens the spiritual sense of students and misguides the public. Why? because it misstates the idea of the divine Principle that you are trying to demonstrate and hides it from the sense of the people. . . . The truth in regard to your Leader heals the sick and saves the sinner."

Such statements from our Leader emphasize the importance of the following By-law in our Church Manual entitled, "Alertness to Duty": "It shall be the duty of every member of this Church to defend himself daily against aggressive mental suggestion, and not be made to forget nor to neglect his duty to God, to his Leader, and to mankind. By his works he shall be judged, — and justified or condemned" (Manual, p. 42).

APPENDIX

A PROPHETIC VISION

APPENDIX

———————————*———————————

A Prophetic Vision

(Copied from the Reminiscences of Mary Baker Eddy by
Judge Septimus J. Hanna, C. S. D.)

In a letter dated May, 1898, Mrs. Eddy speaks of a
vision she had as follows:

. . . Twenty-one years ago, when the first revolt
took place in our church, I had a vision, and uttered it. We then had no funds, I no salary, and
God few followers. In this vision I prophesied
great prosperity, plenty of money, blessings num-
berless, and the utterance was to the Daughter of
Zion: "She shall sit under her own vine and fig
tree, and all peoples shall hear her gladly." That
was when I had but one or two loyal students.
All had deserted in the darkest hour; the people
scorned it, even those I raised instantly from the
dream of death would shun me in the street. In
1898 that dear verse in my hall here was suggested

to my thought, that for fifty years had been forgotten. Oh, the goodness and loving kindness of *our God*! Who can tell it? Oh, the long and still continued nail and spear and: "My God, hast Thou foresaken me?" Oh, the *Love that never faileth*!

Ever lovingly, Mother,

(*Signed*)   Mary Baker Eddy.

Yes, I would publish in Jour. the prophecy you sent.

Verse referred to above:

"Daughter of Zion, awake from thy sadness;
  Awake! for thy foes shall oppress thee no more;
Bright o'er the hills dawns the daystar of gladness;
  Arise! for the night of thy sorrow is o'er."

In 1898 when work had accumulated to such an extent that I wrote Mrs. Eddy for permission to resign some of my places she asked me to adopt a method of relief by taking certain hours each day for self work, during which I was not to be interrupted by anyone for any purpose. She said that had she not adopted such a course she never could have accomplished her work. I did this, and betook myself to the tower of her Commonwealth Avenue residence in Boston, No. 385, which we occupied while I was First Reader of The Mother Church. I called this tower room the "upper chamber". While working here I read as a part of my Bible study the 53d and 54th chapters of Isaiah. As I read the latter it came to me almost as a voice speaking that this chapter was as distinctly and literally a prophecy of Mrs. Eddy as was the 53d chapter a prophecy of Jesus. I continued from day to day to study this chapter in this new light. The more I studied the more firm became the conviction that I was not mistaken in my view of it. I was not, as I then felt and as I now see, emotional or ecstatic on this question, but was governed by a deep spiritual sense of the meaning of the prophecy.

Shortly before I began this study a student had sent in to us a little book entitled "Fragments from the study of a Pastor," written by the Rev. Gardiner Spring, pastor of the Brick Presbyterian Church of New York City, to which reference is made in an article copied further along. This prophecy of Mr. Spring impressed me as being so in line with the prophecy of Isaiah that I read and studied them together.

As a result, I became so imbued with the sense that they both prophesied so distinctly of the Christian Science movement and of Mrs. Eddy that I concluded to prepare an article for publication in our Journal setting forth my convictions, and publishing the "Church in the Wilderness" in connection with the prophecies of Isaiah. I did so and had it set in galley proof, but, of course, would not have published my views without submitting them to Mrs. Eddy and having her approval. In the letter above quoted she wrote immediately before the quoted part, these words: "Yes, the prophecy was wonderful;" then she proceeded to relate her own vision as stated in the letter which I have above quoted. I will now quote from the letters from her in which she referred to my article and the vision of Mr. Spring:

(The prophecy of Mr. Spring is printed in full in Vol. XVI of the *Christian Science Journal*, page 230.)

In a letter dated June 10, 1898, Mrs. Eddy said:

I have not the time to read your article before Laura returns but have seen it enough to say you may have the Vision and the accompanying circumstances at your control. I would make it a *leader* not editorial.

To this she added:

I have read your article 'tis wonderful, *sound*, lawyer-like in argument. Please if you cast this bread on the water add the bit enclosed after fixing it to your liking. God be with us both and He will, *is*.

The following is what Mrs. Eddy added to my article as mentioned in her letter:

We know there is but one God, one Christ Jesus, and one mother of Jesus. But we deem it no infringement to regard the fulfillment of Scripture as indicated at the present period, and named therein, a self-evident proof thereof — not confined to personality but the works which declare the Word.

The next letter I received relating to the article was dated June 18, 1898, which was as follows:

My beloved Student:

The time has not yet come in which to say the wonderful things you have written in proof read by me today, unless you qualify it. Now you may hold your ground as therein, but do not say blandly that I represent the *second appearing of Christ.* That assertion will array mortal mind against us, and M. A. M. has been putting it into your mind to say it, and the infinite Love has *inspired* you *to say it.* Now be wiser than a serpent. Throw out your truths not as affirmations

or protestations, but as suggestions. Then you
catch your fish, and make the wrath of man praise
Him.

                                    With deep love,

(*Signed*)   Mother

June 22nd she again wrote:

Your vision article is too grand, *true*, to be tam-
pered with. I ventured to send for it to see if it
cannot be held together and be the leader, I want
it where all will catch sight of it. I write this before Laura will get here. I am so bothered then
to get time. Will add all else I wish to tell you
after she brings proofs.

Although the last letter indicated permission to proceed
with the publication of the entire article (that is the one I
wrote and the Vision of Mr. Spring) I concluded it best to
publish only that of Mr. Spring and the more general part
of what I said of the prophecy of Isaiah, deferring the
other until a future time and make it a separate article.
After this, events in connection with the work and the
Woodbury suit, came so thick and fast that there seemed
no opportune time to again bring the matter to Mrs.

Eddy's attention (which I felt I must do before publishing it), and there it rested. My own conception of the whole matter, however, has not changed and I see it today just as I saw it then, but I see also that neither our own people, as a whole, nor the outside world were ready for the interpretation of Isaiah then made; and I do not know that they are yet ready.

I here quote the article in full:

EDITOR'S TABLE

It has ever been a peculiarity of human nature to relegate prophecy and prophets to the past. It is as much a truism that a prophet is not without honor save in his own age and generation, as that he is not without honor save in his own country. When the great Prophet of Nazareth appeared on the world's arena, teaching as no prophet had taught before him and proving the efficacy of his teaching by the performance of works that no prophet had performed before him, his age and generation rejected him and his teachings, and refused to believe in the divinity of his works, although compelled to admit that they were wonderful and above all human understanding.

It was easy for that age and generation to believe that Moses, Elijah, and many others who had flourished in previous times, were prophets. Their teachings were unquestionably accepted by the Jews as of divine authority. But to believe that there was actually then amongst them a prophet greater than any who had preceded him was more than the blindness of that age and generation was ready for. Only a few would believe and accept. Yet Jesus' coming had long and repeatedly been foretold, and a Messianic appearing was generally expected among the Jews,—the people who, more than any other, refused to receive him.

A second-coming is as clearly prophesied as was the first coming. The Old Testament writers foretold it, Jesus plainly prophesied it, and the apostles re-iterated these prophecies. The only question among believers in the Bible has been as to the time and manner of the coming. In respect to this there has been, and yet is, much disputation, speculation, and controversy. A personal coming is generally believed in, and the only personality that will at present meet the general expectancy of Christendom is the identical personality of Jesus as he appeared nineteen hundred years ago.

Only, as yet, a comparatively small part of mankind are ready to accept the larger coming comprehended in a re-establishment of the religious *regime* which Jesus inaugurated. This small part of mankind are satisfied that the second-coming has commenced and is now manifesting itself in the works which Jesus taught should be the evidence of the fact that the Kingdom of Heaven was at hand. While this coming is, in a sense, general, presaging a universal Kingdom, it is in another sense individual. There can be no general or universal Kingdom that does not include, first and foremost, the individual. As units make millions and trillions, so individuals make an aggregate. Individuality, therefore, leads to universality. Individuality, in its best sense, includes personality. Not the false personality of mortal sense, but the true personality, which, in its individuality, reflects the Divine character. From this point of view Christian Scientists believe in a personal second-coming.

God has ever manifested Himself, in large measure, through persons or individuals. Through the Biblical writers, and through Moses, Elijah, Abraham, Isaac, Jacob, and many others, He manifested Himself in a sense above and beyond that of the average of their contemporaries or the generality of those who preceded them. In Christ Jesus He manifested Himself in the largest sense of all and in ways apart from all. Yet, as we have said, notwithstanding the wonderful and striking character of such manifesta-

tions, the material perception of that age and generation could not accept them as of God. The "rem-
nant" only could see and accept. It has been so in a
relative sense ever since.

Christian Scientists see in the non-acceptance of
the God-manifestations of today an almost literal repetition of early history. They see a blindness to the
signs of the times which compares well with the ancient blindness. So long has the world been adrift
from the moorings of a genuinely spiritual Christianity that it is not strange it should continue in its self-
mesmerized condition until aroused there from by
special circumstances or proofs of a higher Christianity brought home to individuals in signs and wonders
of healing, and other impressive ways. Until so
awakened, the great majority are indifferent to, and
incredulous of, the tokens of the second-coming.
That thousands are being awakened and are actually
accepting the tokens is, nevertheless, indubitable
proof that convincing circumstances are constantly
taking place. Jesus' saying, "By their fruits ye shall
know them," is becoming more and more a verity.

Must the "Spirit of Truth," or the "Comforter,"
that Jesus said should come be personalized or individualized? Undoubtedly. There could be no fulfillment of prophecy otherwise.

What, then, in the Christian Science estimate, is the second-coming?

First appeared the person or individual. Then followed the works.

Who is the personality or individuality manifesting the second-coming?

The answer of every true Christian Scientist will be: The person or individual who has done, and is doing, the works, in a sense above and beyond that of the average of those, even, who are addressing themselves to the task of regenerating the race.

Is there one such?

Christian Scientists unhesitatingly answer, Yes: The Reverend Mary Baker Eddy.

Where is the proof?

We will produce it. First we go to the Bible. We find our proof in Genesis and Revelation and uniformly between those books.

In the declaration in Genesis that God created man in his own image, male and female, we recognize the divine Fatherhood and Motherhood. That Fatherhood and Motherhood must logically express itself in the male and female. Otherwise there were no true, full "image and likeness." That would not be a complete second-coming which did not express the "fulness of the Godhead bodily." In other words,

there must be a personalized or individualized expression of the male and female of God's creation
before there is a full revelation of God to mankind.
How could such an expression reach human conception unless it were manifested in human form?

By common belief of all Christians Jesus represented the male-hood of God. Is it not reasonable to
assume that a full or completed revelation includes
God's female-hood? If God is male only, it seems
that he would embrace within himself but a half of
Being or Individuality; and it would be impossible to
reconcile such a conception with his own declaration
in Genesis that out of his self-hood he created "male
and female."

Christian Scientists believe in a *full* Godhead; and
thus believing they believe also in a *full* manifestation
of that Godhead to humanity. Therefore they see in
Genesis a prophecy of the second-coming in female
form. In Revelation they see the finality of prophecy. To their understanding the Woman of the
Apocalypse stands in type for the female of God's
creation spoken of in Genesis. They see in spiritual
vision or perception the "Spiritual ideal as a woman
clothed in (reflecting) light, a bride coming down
from heaven, wedded to the Lamb of Love." (Science and Health, p. 561). The Apocalypse is indeed a

"revelation" to their thought, and in it they see a "new heaven and a new earth."

Must the Woman of the Apocalypse be personalized or individualized to mankind? By every principle of logical sequence in Biblical prophecy, Yes.

Without undertaking to speak for any but ourself (the writer hereof), we read in the 54th chapter of Isaiah a distinct prophecy of the personalized or individualized woman spoken of in Genesis and revealed in the Apocalypse. All Bible commentators and students agree that the 53d chapter of Isaiah is directly prophetic of Jesus in his distinctively personal character. We see in the 54th chapter quite as distinct and direct a prophecy of a Woman. Is there not much significance in the fact that the female representing the second-coming should be thus placed in juxtaposition with the male who represented the first coming?

Let us look at this 54th chapter of Isaiah: — "Sing, O barren, thou that didst not bear; break forth into singing, and cry aloud, thou that didst not travail with child: for more are the children of the desolate than the children of the married wife, saith the Lord."

Mary Baker Eddy had only one son born to her of the flesh, and in his early infancy he was surreptitiously taken from her and for years concealed. He has always lived away from her, and yet so lives, although it was her intense desire that he should be with her and be her child in every sense of the word. What mortal sense would call a strange and unaccountable fate has decreed otherwise, and neither son nor mother seems able to control the conditions which have separated them. She is, therefore, to all intents and purposes, without a child of the flesh. But what of her other children, — her spiritual children? They are now numbered by the thousands, and their numbers are being augmented with amazing rapidity; and how spontaneously and unanimously have they arisen and called her "Mother!" Long ere the writer had read the 54th chapter of Isaiah as he now reads it, scarcely knowing why, and like unto a little child, he lisped the word "Mother" when he spoke of her. Thousands of others have done so and thousands more are daily doing so. Among the most touching sights that have ever come within our observation has been the childlike simplicity with which full-grown men — great strong men, physically and mentally — have addressed this delicate, sensitive little woman as "Mother." Not in mockery or jest, but in the seriousness of profound conviction. Yea, her adherents call her their Mother and themselves her children as if by common impulsion, and that impulsion is known to them to be above the human.

"Enlarge the place of thy tent, and let them stretch forth the curtains of thine habitations: spare not, lengthen thy cords, and strengthen thy stakes; for thou shalt break forth on the right hand and on the left; and thy seed shall inherit the Gentiles, and make the desolate cities to be inhabited."

The text-book of Christian Science, "Science and Health with Key to the Scriptures," is but a systematized amplification of the Mosaic Decalogue and the Sermon on the Mount. The teachings of these constitute the groundwork of Christianity. Were they fully understood and practised the Kingdom of Christ would have fully come. To the extent that they are being understood and practised the Kingdom is coming into human consciousness, and the receiving of the Christ-Spirit into human consciousness is the true coming of his Kingdom. Let it always be borne in mind by believers in the Bible that Jesus declared the evidence of the presence of the Kingdom to be the healing of the sick, the casting out of devils, the cleansing of lepers, and the raising of the dead. Certainly these must be the evidences, for, carried to their ultimate effect, they comprehend the complete redemption of the human race.

In so far as these evidences are being now brought into view through Christian Science, may it not be consistently claimed that the second-coming is here; and in so far as a single Woman has been the instrument of bringing these evidences into view, may it not be consistently claimed that she is the personal representative of that second-coming? Is there anything far-fetched or unreasonable in this?

Spiritualization of thought and action is love of God, and love of God is love of the brother. The cords of this love are being rapidly lengthened through Christian Science; the stakes (solid foundation) of this love are being daily strengthened through practical works; literally are the demonstrators of this Science breaking forth on the right hand and on the left, and it requires not the eye of prophecy to see as the necessary result of this breaking forth that the seed "shall inherit the Gentiles (unbelievers), and make the desolate cities (barren aggregates of human thought) to be inhabited." If Christian Science is at all what it claims to be, this prophecy of Isaiah is even now in process of distinct fulfillment. For the verity of its claims its adherents point with confidence to its works.

"Fear not; for thou shalt not be ashamed: neither

be thou confounded; for thou shalt not be put to shame: for thou shalt forget the shame of thy youth, and shalt not remember the reproach of thy widowhood any more. For thy Maker is thine husband; the Lord of hosts is his name; and thy Redeemer the Holy One of Israel; The God of the whole earth shall he be called."

When we recall the reproaches cast upon Mrs. Eddy because of her widowhood, especially by certain of the clergy, and think upon the irrepressible energy with which the tongue of slander has wagged against her, without any known or apparent reason, it is not strange that we read in the tender words of this prophecy God's purpose to protect his child.

Those who are in position to know of the inner life of Mrs. Eddy can most deeply appreciate the last of the above verses. They know that she walks constantly with God, looking to Him for guidance in her every step, and relying upon Him alone for direction in the great religious movement of which she is the head. Deeply was the writer impressed while sitting with her at her dining table in Concord not long since, when in childlike simplicity, yet with deepest seriousness, she said: "I am learning more and more to take God with me into every detail of my life."

If it be possible for "a widow," still living on this

plane of existence, to make her "Maker her hus-band," surely that widow is Mrs. Eddy.

"For the Lord hath called thee as a woman for-saken and grieved in spirit, and a wife of youth, when thou wast refused, saith thy God."

To those familiar with Mrs. Eddy's life and career this is indeed literal prophecy. None could be more so. Alone, and often, in most trying times, forsaken by all but God, she trod the wine-press of her mighty endeavor, undismayedly yet with "bleeding foot-steps," fighting and wrestling and praying against the opposition of the world. A "woman forsaken and grieved in spirit" at times, but rallying quickly in the majesty and might of the Maker who is her husband. And well she might, for, whether she then knew it or not, God had said to her in explicit words, —

"For a small moment have I forsaken thee; but with great mercies will I gather thee."

To those who know, has there not been a startling fulfillment of this prophecy? How often by some has that "small moment" been witnessed, and how quickly have they seen the gathering with great mer-cies.

Not less literally have they witnessed the verifica-tion of this prophecy: —

"In a little wrath I hid my face from thee for a

moment; but with everlasting kindness will I have mercy on thee, saith the Lord thy Redeemer."

Again: — "For this is as the waters of Noah unto me: for as I have sworn that the waters of Noah should no more go over the earth; so have I sworn that I would not be wroth with thee, nor rebuke thee. For the mountains shall depart, and the hills be removed; but my kindness shall not depart from thee, neither shall the covenant of my peace be removed, saith the Lord that hath mercy on thee."

If one who constantly walks with God, who lives the precepts of the Decalogue and the Sermon on the Mount, and who is giving her whole life to the work of enabling others so to live, does not come within these tender assurances, where shalt we find any who do?

"O thou afflicted, tossed with tempest, and not comforted, behold, I will lay thy stones with fair colours, and lay thy foundations with sapphires. And I will make thy windows of agates, and thy gates of carbuncles, and all thy borders of pleasant stones. And all thy children shall be taught of the Lord; and great shall be the peace of thy children. In righteousness shalt thou be established: thou shalt be far from oppression; for thou shalt not fear: and from terror; for it shall not come near thee. . . . No

weapon that is formed against thee shall prosper; and
every tongue that shall rise against thee in judgment
thou shalt condemn.   This is the heritage of the servants of the Lord, and their righteousness is of me,
saith the Lord."

Could there be a more explicit fulfillment of this
prophecy than the following, written by Mrs. Eddy to
the writer, but with no reference whatever to the use
we are now making of it, and not intended for publication at all, until by special request consent was obtained?

"Twenty-one years ago, when the first revolt took
place in our church, I had a vision and uttered it.
We then had no funds, I no salary, and Christian
Science few followers.   In that vision I prophesied
great prosperity, plenty of money, blessings unnumbered; and the utterance was to the 'Daughter of
Zion; she shall sit under her own vine and fig-tree,
and all peoples shall hear her gladly.'   That was
when I had but one or two loyal students, all had
deserted in the darkest hour, the people scorned my
teaching, and even those I raised instantly from the
door of death would shun me on the street.   In 1898
that dear verse in my hall at Concord was suggested
to my thought which, for fifty years, had been forgotten: —

"Daughter of Zion, awake from thy sadness;
　Awake! for thy foes shall oppress thee no more.
　Bright o'er thy hills dawns the day-star of gladness;
　Arise! for the night of thy sorrow is o'er."

She closes her letter with these words:

"Oh, the goodness and loving kindness of our God,
　who can tell it?
Oh, the Love that never faileth!"

Millions are now hearing the "Daughter of Zion" gladly. She is sitting under her own vine and fig-tree; God has prospered her and her Cause most bounteously in the financial and every other rightful way; she who was "afflicted, tossed with tempest, and (for a small moment) not comforted," has literally witnessed the rich fulfillment of God's promise to her: "I will lay thy stones with fair colours, and lay thy foundations with sapphires. And I will make thy windows of agates, and thy gates of carbuncles, and all thy borders of pleasant stones." Literally enough has this promise been redeemed in the material sense, but with overflowing abundance in the spiritual — present and prospective.

But what of this material abundance? To no selfish

end is it being appropriated. It is fast being converted into the Lord's treasury. Such use is being
made of it as would be expected of one who in prophetic vision foresaw "prosperity, plenty of money,
and blessings unnumbered," for a sacred Cause.

In the April, 1898, *Journal*, Mrs. Eddy, speaking
of the financial problem as she experienced it, says:

"After four years from my discovery of Christian
Science, while taking no remuneration for my labors,
and healing all manner of diseases, I was confronted
with the fact of no monetary means left wherewith to
hire a hall in which to speak, or to establish a *Christian Science Home* for indigent students (which I
yearned to do), or even to meet my own current expenses, and halted from necessity.

"I had cast my all into the treasury of Truth, but
where were the means with which to carry on a
Cause? To desert the Cause never occurred to me,
but nobody then wanted Christian Science, nor gave
it a half penny. Though sorely oppressed I was
above begging, and knew well the priceless worth of
what had been bestowed without money or price.
Just then God stretched forth His hand. He it was
that bade me do what I did, and it prospered at every
step. . . . It was thus that I earned the means
wherewith to start a *Christian Science Home* for the

poor worthy student, to establish a *Metaphysical College*, to plant our first magazine, to purchase the site for a church edifice, to give my church the *Christian Science Journal*, and to keep the 'wolves in sheep's clothing,' from preying upon my pearls, from clogging the wheels of Christian Science."

The donation of the valuable lot of ground to The Mother Church in Boston, liberal aid to the erection of the church building, countless contributions to indigent students and to charitable purposes outside our ranks, a score of contributions to branch churches and societies for building and other purposes, the transfer *in toto* of the Publishing Society with all its property, perquisites, and prospects, as well as her valuable residence on Commonwealth Avenue, to The Mother Church in perpetuity, and her latest donation in trust of four thousand dollars to the children of Scientists or "Busy Bees," — these are *some* of the evidences of the sense in which this Daughter of Zion is sitting under her own vine and fig-tree and dispensing the wine of Life and the figs of Love to hungering and thirsting humanity.

This God-fearing, God-loving, and God-reflecting woman truly is witnessing the reassuring and unmistakable evidences that her children are being "taught of the Lord." She can easily foresee that when they shall have imbibed and practised the fulness of such teaching "great will be the peace" of her "children."

Has not this Daughter of Zion also witnessed the fulfillment of this promise of God: "No weapon that is formed against thee shall prosper"?

Every form of opposition has been made against her and her teaching possible to humanity, saving only attempts to murder her in the ordinary or physical sense. The mental assassin has exhausted his ingenuity and resources in his vain efforts. But no weapon raised against her has prospered. Grandly and majestically has her work gone on, and mightily has it prospered. So much so that it is challenging the wonder and awe of the millions.

We shall not stop to enlarge upon the "mighty works." They are becoming well known and widely recognized. Read of some of them in this *Journal*, and in the newspapers and magazines of the country. Hear of them in the weekly testimonial meetings. Hear how thousands have been raised from beds of sorrow, sickness, and pain, to joy, and health, and hope; how despairing sinners have been aroused from the lethargy of hades to a sense of their manhood in Christ Jesus and their childhood in God; how agnostics have become unquestioning believers in the Divine power to heal and save; how atheists have come to *know* that God *is*, and that in Him they live, and move, and have their being; how infidels have been reclaimed from all unbelief; how sceptics have become convinced by proof they could no longer dispute; how drunkards have been redeemed from hells of woe and made to rejoice in freedom from their dread tormentor; how licentiates and libertines have been made to blush for their sins and turned toward abstinence and purity; how dishonesty is being made to quail and cringe before the majesty of Truth and Right; how hate and selfishness are being supplanted by self-sacrifice and love; how all the blighting and damning qualities of human thought are being uprooted and destroyed to the purification and spiritualization of such thought; and how those who have only recently been the unhappy victims of some or all of these death-dealing trammels are now proving their disenthralment by healing their neighbors of sickness and pointing the way to their salvation from sin, whilst healer and healed, saver and saved, are alike coming into the temple of the New Jerusalem, literally "leaping and shouting, and praising God."

Observe too, how rapidly beautiful and stately church edifices, reared in the name of, and dedicated

to, the God of the living, not of the dead, are spring-
ing into existence all over our land; how one common sermon, compiled from the Eternal Word, is
preached in more than five hundred places in this
country, England, and the Continental countries
each recurring Sabbath, while the number is being
almost weekly added to; how reading, and hearing
these sermons read, are healing sickness and awakening sinners every Sabbath day; how the reading of the
Bible and the books whose writing was divinely entrusted to the "Woman's" hand, is daily healing sickness and saving sinners; how the Spirit of God,
through these manifold instrumentalities, is indeed
moving upon the face of the troubled waters of mortal discord to the calming thereof, and how the Light
whereof God said, Let it *be*, and it *was*, is shining
athwart the world's horizon and glinting into the
darkest recesses of mortal thought, — observe and
think upon all this, and say: Is not "this the heritage
of the servants of the Lord," and is not "their righteousness" of Him?

While, in the foregoing, we plainly see the
Woman, as in other Scripture we see the Man, we
look beyond all personality and as plainly see the
Male and Female, — the universal Manhood and
Womanhood comprehended in the Divine scheme,

— and know that the ideal Manhood and Womanhood of God's Word personally typified as we have shown, is, — must in the Divine order be, — the heritage of every son and daughter of God's creating; and he created *all*.

Hence we recognize personality in type only that we may thereby understand the unified Individuality of Father and Son, and Mother and Daughter, in the fulness of that Godhead whose second-coming is upon us, wherein we see "a new Heaven and a new earth." We see the man who was "despised and rejected of men; a man of sorrows, and acquainted with grief . . . oppressed and afflicted;" and we see also the Man of whom God said: "Therefore will I divide him a portion with the great, and he shall divide the spoil with the strong; because he hath poured out his soul unto death; and he was numbered with the transgressors; and he bare the sins of many, and made intercession for the transgressors" (Isaiah, 53).

We see also the woman of travail, spoken of in Isaiah, as before shown, and of whom God further spoke in Jeremiah, 4: "For I have heard a voice as of a woman in travail, and the anguish as of her that bringeth forth her first child, the voice of the daughter of Zion, that bewaileth herself, that spreadeth her hands, saying, Woe is me *now*! [italics are ours] for

my soul is wearied because of murderers;" and we
see also the Woman of whom God said: "Who hath
heard such a thing? who hath seen such things?
Shall the earth be made to bring forth in one day? or
shall a nation be born at once? for as soon as Zion
travailed, she brought forth her children" (Isaiah,
66). "Behold, the Lord hath proclaimed unto the
end of the world, Say ye to the daughter of Zion,
Behold, thy salvation cometh" (Isaiah, 62). And we
read of the man and woman: "For your shame ye
shall have double; and for confusion they shall rejoice in their portion: therefore in their land they
shall possess the double: everlasting joy shall be unto
them . . . . And I will direct their work in truth,
and I will make an everlasting covenant with them.
And their seed shall be known among the Gentiles,
and their offspring among the people: all that see
them shall acknowledge them, that they are the seed
which the Lord hath blessed." (Isaiah, 61).

By way of epilogue to this effort to "render tribute
where tribute is due," and, in some small part, meet
the imperative demands of the history of our times,
we present herewith what seems to us a remarkable
prophecy; a prophecy in direct line with the Scripture prophecies to which we have above referred.
Nor let us sneer at the author's claim that this proph-

ecy came to him as a vision and by apparently super-
natural means. Until we know more of God and his
methods let us withhold our feeble, finite judgment,
— unless we are ready to acknowledge that God
does, in these latter days, speak to his faithful ones
through vision and voice as he did of old. We refer
to an article entitled, "The Church in the Wilderness," contained in a little book written in 1838 by
the Rev. Gardiner Spring, Pastor of the Brick Presbyterian Church of New York, the work itself being
entitled, "Fragments from the Study of a Pastor."

We should like to make some comments on this, to
us wonderful, production, but space will not permit.
Let it be observed, however, that some of the Scriptural quotations are from the 54th of Isaiah.

It may be interesting to know how this somewhat
ancient little book came to light at this *particular
time*, and we will mention how.

A faithful student of Mrs. Eddy's sent it us,
saying: —

"I would like to tell you how the book came into
my hands. It is interesting to know how it came to
light. Two years ago last winter I was living in a
furnished house which I rented of a dear friend.
There was in the house a large number of books
which once belonged to an old uncle. I used to sit

by a window when reading; close to this window stood a small bookcase filled mostly with small old books. Two or three times, perhaps oftener, when sitting there the thought came, I wonder if there is not something among those books that would give light on the Bible, or explain its truth, and would say, Sometime I will look the books over. One morning I was sorely tempted; after the morning's work was finished I sat down with Science and Health to dispel the seeming error. I had read but a short time when the thought again came that there might be something in the bookcase of value. I looked at the books, took one out; the first or second — I cannot remember which — was 'The Church in the Wilderness.' I commenced reading in the middle of the chapter, but the little I read healed me. The next day as soon as I returned from church I read the whole chapter. I then invited the students up to read it. When I read it a year from that time I saw far more than at first.

"I am filled with gratitude that I reflected God sufficiently to bring to light this marvelous history of the appearing of Truth. It helped me to realize what our Mother is, as never before, for I knew I was reading of her experiences. Also those of The Mother Church."

"The Mother Church" is the material expression of that church universal implied in the second-coming; but we ask, in all sincerity, could that Church have been thus expressed but for the labor, toil, and self-sacrificing devotion of the Daughter of Zion to whom its building was entrusted?

The prophet Isaiah clearly saw the personalized Woman. The Bible commentators, not discerning the fact of a female appearing as the type of the second-coming, naturally enough saw in Isaiah's prophecy only the Church of Christ, apart from any particular person.

Christian Scientists recognize in the material structure, called "The Mother Church" — The First Church of Christ, Scientist, in Boston, Mass., with its branches throughout the world, the type of the second-coming of the Christ, or the final and universal application of the Christ-Principle. They also recognize in the Founder of this Church the typical embodiment in human form of the female of God's creation prophesied in Scripture.

These are evidences presented to mortal sense of the universal idea of the Church and of the Woman embraced in Revelation.

Our latter-day prophet, the Rev. Gardiner Spring, saw also both the Church, and the Woman typifying the Church. Hence its impressiveness from the standpoint of Scientific prophecy.

It is interesting to note that the place of Mr. Spring's revelation was on *Mont Viso* (Mount of Vision) of the Alpine range, at a point whereon the persecuted *Vaudois* or Waldenses, found an asylum. It will be remembered that this sect arose in the south of France about A. D. 1170. They were the first to protest, as a body, against the corruption of the Roman church, and as a consequence were, of course, bitterly persecuted. Persecution, however (as it always does), gave vitality to their doctrines, which passed on to Wycliffe and Huss, and through them produced the Reformation in Germany and England. This sect was distinguished from the Franciscans in that they taught the *doctrine* of Christ, while the latter taught the *person* of Christ, or Jesus. They had no *official priesthood*. They regarded the sacraments as merely symbolical, and with them ceremonies gradually disappeared. They became merged in the general Protestant movement in Germany and England.

As will be readily seen by Christian Scientists, they were among the forerunners of the larger Protestantism which is finding its expression in a general protest against all forms and conditions of erroneous doctrine, — in the churches and out of them.

The following was added by Mrs. Eddy: — "We know there is but one God, one Christ Jesus, and one mother of Jesus. But we deem it no infringement to regard the fulfillment of Scripture as indicated at the present period, and named therein, a self-evident proof thereof — not confined to personality but the works which declare the Word."

(The prophecy of Mr. Spring is printed in full in Vol. XVI of the *Christian Science Journal*, page 230.)

INDEX

ANIMAL MAGNETISM, 98, 105, 110, 179, 181, 254.

ANTHONY, DAVID, named Director, 1889, 61.

ARMSTRONG, JOSEPH, 144, 145; manager of Christian Science Publishing Society, 94; appointed Director, 94; author, 97.

BARRETT, W. F., raised from Dead, 117.

BARTLETT, JULIA S., 39, 40; Christian Science practitioner, 6; meeting in her rooms accepts new trust deed for the Church, 1892, 91.

BIBLE LESSONS, vi, 39, 40, 138, 146, 147, 219; duties of Committee, 165.

BIBLE REFERENCES, Acts, 222, 229; 231, 241; Angel Gabriel, 220; Babylonish woman, 194; baptism of the eunuch, 231; Bethlehem, 210, 217; Corinthians, 109, 207, 222, 230; Daniel, 188–190, 242, 249, 250; Deuteronomy, 209; Door of the sheepfold, 211, 212; Elijah, 227, 228, 230, 271; Ezekiel, 187, 212, 221, 230; Galatians, 118; Genesis, 84, 187, 209, 221, 225, 226, 240, 243, 249, 259, 275, 276; Gog and Magog, 230; Hebrews, 204, 210, 221, 222, 226, 238; Holy City, 221, 222; Immaculate Conception, 205; Isaiah, 192, 209, 243, 244, 267, 271, 277, 280, 290, 291; James, 214; Jeremiah, 41; Jesus, 205, 206–208, 210–215, 217, 218, 222, 223, 224, 228, 229, 272; Jesus, and Peter, 59, and Christ defined, 155; Job, 98; John, 156, 158, 173, 206, 207, 210, 211, 213, 215, 224, 239, 244, 245, 247, 248; —the Baptist, 210, 238, 239; John on Patmos, 223; Joshua, 177; kingdom of heaven, 207; II Kings, 228; Lamb of God, 210; light, 209–211, 214, 216; Lazarus, 220; Lord's Prayer, 96; Luke, 75, 127, 176, 182, 187,196, 215, 220, 230, 238–241, 244, 245; man born blind, 206; Mark, 181, 194; Matthew, 175, 185, 186, 197, 199, 206, 207, 228; Micah, 217, 223, 247, 248, 259, 260; Moses, 180, 204, 205, 208, 209, 222, 226, 227, 228, 238, 271; Noah, 228, 283; Old Testament, 186, 272; Paul, 98, 110, 159, 164, 179, 207, 222, 230; Pentecostal Day, 228, 229; Peter, 155, 173, 206, 207, 222; Philip, 231; Psalms, 23, 37, 41, 157, 243; promised Comforter, 223; raising from Dead, 120; Revelation, 58, 84, 148, 150, 157, 158, 168, 174, 185, 188, 189, 197–199, 208, 217, 223, 230, 246, 249, 250–253, 255, 257, 258,

ELDER, SAMUEL J., declares Manual legal, 137.

FAITH, 237, 238, 239.

FARLOW, ALFRED, answers attacks, 115; general manager of the Committee on Publication, 115, 116.

"FIRST MEMBERS," v, 31, 99, 163; selected by Mrs. Eddy, 3; accept new deed for Church, 1892, 90–92; twelve students voted as, 1892, 92; listed, 92; control of Church business taken away, 123; discontinued, 167.

FOSTER, DR. E. J. (see also Eddy, Dr. Foster), 22, 23, 27; adopted by Mrs. Eddy in 1888, 21.

FRYE, CALVIN A., 6, 22, 27, 44; letter to Mr. Knapp, 15, 16; goes to Concord, N.H., 37; helped by Mrs. Eddy, 118–120.

GRAGG, ELDORA O., Second Reader, 101.

GREENE, EUGENE H., 63; named Director, 1889, 61.

HANNA, JUDGE SEPTIMUS J., 42, 43, 107, 130–131, 143, 192, 193, 261, 265; First Reader, 101, 267; letter to Bliss Knapp, 1918, 141; bible study, 267; vision article, 271–297.

HANNA, MRS. SEPTIMUS J., 146, 152.

HARRIS, MRS. MARY E., 6, 7; heals Mrs. Knapp, 8.

HARVARD COLLEGE, v.

HASTINGS, LEBBEUS, 4, 5.

HEALING, 38, 216, 238–239, 242; for deafness, 10; opium, 11; by Mr. Knapp, 31; by Mrs. Knapp, 107–109; of Bliss Knapp, 112; of opposition by Mr. Farlow, 116; by Mr. Kimball, 117; by Mrs.Eddy, 118; techniques, 119, 120; acknowledged as essential function of the Church, 166; how accomplished, 180; witness of divine mission, 257.

HEBREW, 216, 217, 225

"HISTORY OF THE MOTHER CHURCH", 144.

HYMNS, "Joy Cometh in the Morning," 28, 29.

JOHNSON, WILLIAM B., 39, 97, 144; named Director, 1889, 61; loyal to Mrs. Eddy, 75; tests his faith in supply, 76; warns of plot to divert Church funds, 77; "First Member," letter to Mrs. Knapp, 90; named Director of Church, 1892, 91–92.

KIMBALL, EDWARD A., 129, 261; healed, 1887, 116; Board of Lectureship, 116; heals, 117.

KNAPP, AARON, 4.

KNAPP, BLISS, 36, 44, 110; letter from Mrs. Eddy, v, vi; meets Mrs. Eddy, 25; healed, 112; letter from Mrs. Eddy, 1906, 135; letter from Judge Hanna, 141.

KNAPP, DAPHNE, 3, 12, 22, 24, 28, 44.